Challenge Thinking and Deepen Understanding

Challenge Thinking and Deepen Understanding

The Instructional Approach for Implementing the Common Core Standards, Grades 3–12

Lisa A. Fisher

ROWMAN & LITTLEFIELD
Lanham • Boulder • New York • Toronto • Plymouth, UK

Published by Rowman & Littlefield
4501 Forbes Boulevard, Suite 200, Lanham, Maryland 20706
www.rowman.com

10 Thornbury Road, Plymouth PL6 7PP, United Kingdom

Copyright © 2014 by Lisa A. Fisher

All rights reserved. No part of this book may be reproduced in any form or by any electronic or mechanical means, including information storage and retrieval systems, without written permission from the publisher, except by a reviewer who may quote passages in a review.

British Library Cataloguing in Publication Information Available

Library of Congress Cataloging-in-Publication Data

Fisher, Lisa A., 1980–
  Challenge thinking and deepen understanding : the instructional approach for implementing the common core standards, grades 3–12 / Lisa A. Fisher.
    pages cm
  Includes bibliographical references.
  ISBN 978-1-4758-0854-4 (cloth) — ISBN 978-1-4758-0855-1 (pbk.) — ISBN 978-1-4758-0856-8 (electronic) 1. Reading. 2. Reading comprehension. 3. Content area reading. 4. Language arts—United States—Standards. I. Title.

  LB1050.F48 2014
  372.4—dc23   2014001080

Contents

List of Figures		vii
List of Tables		ix
Foreword by Dr. Nancy Williams		xi
Preface		xv
Acknowledgments		xix
1	Understand Reading Closely: Multiple Interactions with Text	1
2	Open the Mind with Change Perspective: A Reading Closely Approach	15
3	Actively Read with Preview/Review	33
4	Game Changer with Strategic Approach	49
5	Stretch into High Cognitive Literacy Tasks	63
6	Multiple Interactions with Literary Texts	75
Appendices		89
Professional References		127
Literature References		129
About the Author		131

Figures

Figure 1.1. Overview Reading Closely and Writing Purposefully Options — 12

Figure 2.1. Change Perspective Expert Read Highlighting Key — 28

Tables

Table 2.1.	Optional Reading Closely Perspectives for Informational Text	21
Table 2.2.	Evidence for Change Perspective Sample Lesson	30
Table 3.1.	Types of Test Structures	39
Table 3.2.	Sample Writing Response Rubric	46
Table 5.1.	Sample Lesson for Analyzing Craft and Structure	73
Table 6.1.	Optional Reading Closely Perspectives for Literary Text	78

Foreword

When ancient cultures engaged in battle, one man was assigned to carry the flag, an honor that resulted in the encouragement of soldiers to fight for their cause or country. This concept of standard-bearer has continued and evolved throughout history with applications to many professions, including education, with the intent not to battle—but rather to provide quality guidelines. Interestingly, professional educators throughout our nation's history have held their students to high standards with or without mandates. These standard-bearers planned and implemented lessons that prepared citizens who could easily function in their communities in particular, and in society in general. In relatively recent times this criterion has gradually become more universal with the advent of professional and national standards.

During the past four decades as an educator (classroom teacher, supervisor, university professor, and department chair), I have personally witnessed the proverbial pendulum of change swing from the freedom of the open classroom philosophies of the early '70s to a highly structured scripted reading program of the late '70s–early '80s. The pattern continued when whole language blossomed in the '90s and was quickly replaced by the findings of the National Reading Panel and the implementation of the No Child Left Behind Act of 2001. This increase in standards and mandates has now developed into the Common Core Standards, which are becoming ensconced in our schools today.

The initiation of the Common Core State Standards has caused confusion among teachers, frustration among school administrators, and a political battle between vocal members of the left and the right. Some are concerned about the eventual "Test" and the idea that we are indeed testing our children too much. Some are concerned about government's overreach in an effort to make all children "common" and the possible "dumbing down of the curriculum." As I write this foreword, government officials in Florida are in the midst of holding a variety of hearings to determine the future of the Common Core, a practice consistent with other states (Alabama, Georgia, Oklahoma, and Utah).

Most educators—including both reading teachers and teachers of reading—would agree that standards do indeed guide us and that a sense of commonality does assist planning and implementation of teaching reading across the curriculum, but they are often uncertain of practice. This is particularly true of elementary-prepared teachers who take several reading and assessment courses but sometimes have limited exposure to reading in the content areas, an emphasis of Common Core and the use of expository texts. Yet some educators claim that fictional works play a second fiddle in instruction and are skeptical of how this limited utilization of genre may play out in classroom practice.

Regardless of your position regarding the rollout of these new standards, some core principles should remain and indeed have been championed by excellent teachers who have held on to their standards throughout their teaching career—even if it meant closing their classroom doors (and away from the eyes and ears of quality checkers) to teach in the ways they know best. These teachers recognize the tenets of reading instruction and the concept of understanding should dominate the conversation, and as a result, the curriculum. They have also not "bought into" the "swinging pendulum theory" and "thrown out all previous philosophies," but have realized that by standing on the shoulders of the curriculum giants who came before, they can view a clearer appreciation of the Common Core Standards.

Lisa Fisher is one of those educators. As an accomplished teacher and "teacher of teachers," she has held on to standards that she knew worked with reading teachers and teachers of reading. As such, she has written a thoughtful book, which will assist both novice and experienced teachers. Novices will read practical descriptions of the Common Core Standards with a better understanding, while the experienced teacher will sigh with relief of familiarity when they acknowledge that they have always practiced these strategies. Further, explanations of the Common Core Standards are clarified through illustration of a sixth grade unit, which weaves reading practices with the content areas of math and science. This instructional context for the implementation of the Common Core Standards will become a framework for novices and experienced teachers to plan and implement additional lessons that will meet these new mandates and motivate students.

We all agree (at least I hope we do) that our children need to be prepared for an ever-changing world, and Lisa Fisher offers a comprehensive view of how teachers may achieve this goal without compromising the philosophies of the heroes who guided their instructional practices. By standing on the shoulders of giants, and armed with the practical applications as presented by Lisa Fisher, teachers can lead their students on a successful path in this ever-changing world. Finally, this text will prompt all educators to recall what the core of good teaching is and what is common among good teachers.

—Dr. Nancy Williams

Preface

With each day, I am reminded of my struggles as a reader. I have to work extra hard to be prepared to use text in professional learning and/or with students in a classroom. There are always words I am not familiar with, but I have something I hope to inspire in every single student—perseverance and resilience. That is the secret to successfully tackling literacy difficulties. As an educator, I stand proud to advocate for all students and have written this professional text on their behalf. I understand what it feels like to struggle with text, so the ideas suggested throughout this text, I have used myself as a reader and as a teacher working with students over the past ten years.

I have taught at every level of education (elementary, middle, high school, and college). Through these experiences, I have observed and instructed a large age group of students. In my years of teaching and providing professional learning for educators, I have realized a huge need to help students who are more likely to struggle or be reluctant learners to read with greater ease and enjoyment. I want to help those who feel like throwing a book through a wall and breaking down with tears because they fumble over every other word. Although I agree nothing in life is worth having if you haven't worked for it, I also agree students should not feel like they want to quit being a lifelong learner by the end of elementary school.

More importantly, I have learned the only way to get better at reading is to read and read again. Good readers do not just read a text one time, but again and again in order to gain a deeper understanding of the meaning. This text has grown out of the dirt of trial and error and hard work. We are our students' voices, and we must advocate for them to fight the battle of literacy another day. It is never too late to become literate and thrive in a twenty-first-century world of multiple literacies all around you.

With new standards adopted by forty-four states and the District of Columbia, this professional text will address strategies to utilize in order to master the Common Core State Standards with reading closely to deepen understanding of informational text. This professional text offers why and what the English/Language Arts (ELA) Common Core State Standards (CCSS) are, how to implement strategies aligned with the standards, and the importance behind text complexity and rigor. All of the strategies can be used no matter what standards are being taught and in any discipline.

The first chapter explains how and why CCSS are a part of future educational endeavors and explains the purpose of all the other chapters, which focuses readers to specifically discover how to help students read closely and purposefully to deepen comprehension of informational text. Readers will discover where to start with reading closely and how to build rigor with texts and tasks through the implementation of three literacy approaches (*Change Perspective*, *Preview/Review*, and *Strategic Approach*). This focus helps move students toward mastery of all College and Career Readiness Anchor Standards for Reading Informational Texts, as well as thrive in society.

The second chapter delves deep into the first approach to reading closely, change perspective. In this chapter readers will discover what this approach looks like and sounds like at the secondary level in order to help bring reading alive for all students. It is a highly engaging approach that encourages students to be critical readers of informational text or all multiliteracies (e.g., social media, advertisements, Internet sites, etc.).

The next chapter increases in rigor and has students sweep through a text multiple times for several different reasons, each building on the one before in order to deepen understanding and answer challenging questions using text evidence. This approach, preview/review, guides teachers and students through a systematic way to look at text for the purpose of extracting information, using text as evidence, and critically think about multiliteracies.

Chapter 4 addresses the most complicated approach to reading closely, strategic approach. This chapter helps teachers take students on a journey through text using text marking, categorization, and drawing conclusions. It is the most difficult approach for teachers to implement and the most difficult for students, but the end result is students learning to tear text apart, put it back together, and extract critical information to develop new understanding within their own learning process.

The following chapter helps teachers utilize text for a third and fourth read. Teachers will help students dig into the semantics (word choice) of the syntax (sentence structure) in order to truly analyze and critique author's tone, purpose, perspective, and position in relation to other sources. Students will compare and contrast these skills across multiliteracies as they develop into critical readers. They will ask why authors used certain words and why authors chose to present information in a certain way (objective versus subjective). When students begin to look at the sentences and how they are constructed by word choice in relationship to all other sentences, then they can truly develop an understanding of information presented by multiple sources in order to form their own opinions and beliefs about the world around them.

In the final chapter, readers will discover how to take the approaches addressed in chapters 2 through 5 and use them with literary text. Educators will learn how to help students view literary text in different ways, interact with literary text, and study word choice and literary design to deepen reading of several genres.

Therefore, this text is for any educator thriving in the 3–12 education lifestyle and wishes to inspire each and every student to walk away from text with a greater understanding of ideas and ready to use their new understanding to collaborate with others, communicate effectively, think critically about the world around them, and thrive in a future unknown with creativity. Let the interaction of multiple literacies drive what you do each and every day.

Acknowledgments

This professional text would not be possible if not for the support and guidance of many knowledgeable people. First, I wish to express my gratitude to Dr. Nancy Williams for teaching me to be a literacy leader and working with me to write the foreword for this book. She has dedicated so much of her personal time in helping me get this book completed.

Dr. Nancy Williams earned a Ph.D. in curriculum and instruction from Louisiana State University, an M.Ed. in early childhood education from the University of South Alabama, and a B.S. in elementary education from Worcester State College (Massachusetts). Additionally, she completed graduate work at the University of South Alabama that led to state certification in reading, supervision, and administration.

Dr. Williams is a former elementary school teacher and administrator and has been an assistant professor at the University of North Carolina at Charlotte and at the University of Houston. She was awarded tenure and promoted to associate professor at the University of Houston, and after serving the institution for six years, she became the chair of the Education Department at Cedar Crest College in Allentown, Pennsylvania. She then accepted the position of associate professor at the University of South Florida, where she was awarded tenure and received an award for excellent teaching at the undergraduate level.

At all of these institutions, she served the university, community, and the profession. She advised students at all levels, served on numerous committees, volunteered in schools, and offered her expertise as a reviewer and editor for several literacy journals and annuals. Her research interests include vocabulary teaching and learning, motivation and authentic reading and writing, and literacy across the curriculum. She is a frequent presenter at the American Educational Research Association, the Association of Literacy Research, the International Reading Association, and the American Reading Forum.

I also would like to thank my husband, Ryan, who is not only an exceptional instructional leader but also a fabulous and supportive husband. Thank you, Ryan, for understanding my ongoing need to research, write, and share my love for teaching reading with anyone and everyone who will listen. He gave up so much time to read each chapter and provide some feedback that is invaluable.

In addition, this book would not be possible without the examples and scenarios of my friends and colleagues: Andrea Altman and Donna College. Each one attended trainings and observed sample lessons in order to provide wonderful additions to the text, making it the descriptive book it has developed into over the past three years. Thank you so very much for your help with this process.

Of course, I want to thank my agent, Bertram Linder, who helped me grow in my thinking about this text and for believing in my ideas to continuously send it out day after day until someone said yes. I would not be anywhere without his ongoing persistence.

Similarly, I want to thank Thomas Koerner, vice president and editorial director at R & L Education, who saw enough in my words to publish yet another book by me. After a decade of trial and error, feedback from students, ongoing learning, and continuous collegial discussion, my brain continues to stretch and grow full of thoughts and ideas that I get to share with the world.

Consequently, the guidance and support received from all the people who contributed and who continue to spread the word are vital for the success of this text. I am grateful for their constant support and help.

Chapter One

Understand Reading Closely
Multiple Interactions with Text

For a few years, a group of teachers have done the same thing to students; they have taught units from a textbook page by page. At the end of each year, the state assessment results yield similar outcomes—50 percent to 80 percent of students are considered proficient at affluent schools and 25 percent to 55 percent of students are considered proficient at other schools.

This continuous input and output cycle drives teachers' morale down, yet they do not know what to do to get different results. It appears as though everything and everyone is to blame except the key pieces that schools actually have control over—intentional planning from standards that includes ongoing progress monitoring through formative assessments to measure response to learning and problem solving when students do not respond how teachers intended them to respond.

Therefore, there comes a time when change must take place. This type of inevitable change may not always be welcomed with open arms and a great big smile, but it is shaping and molding the future whether you like it or not. That is what the Common Core State Standards (CCSS) are doing for forty-four states and the District of Columbia, hundreds of thousands of educators, and hundreds of thousands of students and parents across the United States of America, but no matter what standards you teach, the process is always the same. Whether states are going with these standards or sticking with their own, it is time to ask why and do what is best for students.

There are two ways you can view any type of change. You can be negative and put forth resistance, or you can be positive and put forth willingness. However, either path you choose, the change is still happening. So let's assume you will choose the latter because you understand that this is not really about you, but it is about the students who walk through your classroom door each and every day. That is where this text will help you make the necessary changes for the high expectations of the CCSS or any set of standards, no matter what subject you teach.

Simply implementing new standards will not close the learning gap amongst students, but changing instruction and curriculum based on students' responses to teaching aligned with CCSS or grade level standards will put education on a better path. This will require knowing the standards and planning for purposeful and meaningful learning to take place. This will require students to experience multiple interactions with the world around them.

THE WHY BEHIND THE COMMON CORE STATE STANDARDS

You want to start by understanding the reason for the adoption of the CCSS by so many states. Every state was educating students on their own standards. Some states' standards were considered easy and some more difficult, but they certainly were not equal. Although there is still much debate on which states will fully implement, the premise behind the need for common expectations across our nation needs to be a priority.

In 2006, ACT published the 2005 assessment data in a report, *Reading between the Lines: What the ACT Reveals about College Readiness in Reading*, that indicated students are not adequately prepared to read text at the college level nor the career level. "Only 51 percent of ACT-tested high school graduates met ACT's College Readiness Benchmark for Reading, demonstrating their readiness to handle the reading requirements for typical credit-bearing first-year college coursework, based on the 2004-2005 results of the ACT" (ACT, 2006, p. 9).

In addition, the National Assessment of Educational Progress (NAEP, 2011) conducted a study of student performance of fourth and eighth grade students in reading. In comparison to 2009, the 2011 results indicated no significant change in student performance, although for educators watching high-stakes assessment results come in each year, this may be nothing new.

So several stakeholders, such as David Coleman, the Council of Chief State School Officers, the National Governors Association Center for Best Practices, and Susan Pimentel, just to name a few, got together to lead the collaborative effort with states to establish a set of new standards for English/Language Arts (ELA) and Mathematics with high expectations and rigor for all students. They also included literacy standards for Social Studies/History, Science, and Technical Subjects with the intent of embedding reading, writing, listening and speaking, and language across the disciplines.

It is important for you to know this is not a federally controlled effort, but the federal government does help fund the effort. New standards are created and refined by the states. This means states participated in editing and revising the CCSS, providing feedback, asking questions, and challenging what did not make sense in order to ensure education gets it right this time so students do not move between states, resulting in holes in skills and knowledge. However, instead of starting from kindergarten and building up, they started with college and career skills that are needed and worked back—planning with the end in mind, just like teachers are supposed to do for their curriculum and instruction implementation aligned with grade level expectations (standards).

"Building on the excellent foundation of standards states have laid, the Common Core State Standards are the first step in providing our young people with a high-quality education" (Common Core State Standards Initiative, 2012). With Florida teaching toward the same expectations as Georgia and then being assessed with the same high-stakes assessment, educators can no longer say scores are low because our expectations are higher, or because our tests are more difficult. Instead, it should inspire collegial conversations focused on what is being done right, what is not working, and how do you know?

THE STRUCTURE OF CCSS
ENGLISH/LANGUAGE ARTS

For the purpose of this text, you will only continue your learning around the idea of the English/Language Arts (ELA) Common Core State Standards (CCSS), but really reading closely is applicable for any set of standards. It is beyond the realm of this text to break down or unpack each standard, but instead it will help you understand instructional strategies you can use to align curriculum and instruction with grade level standards across core content areas and in life.

Like most language arts standards, the ELA CCSS have four strands (Reading, Writing, Speaking and Listening, and Language). Each strand has College and Career Readiness (CCR) anchor standards. This is the end in mind for all students. In addition, each strand has grade level specific standards aligned with the CCR anchor standards to help move the students along a progression of learning toward proficiency of the standards. In the first and second set of grade bands (K–2 and 3–5), there are also Foundational Skills that must be explicitly taught and purposefully practiced (print concepts, phonological awareness, phonics and word recognition, and fluency), although fluency is something continually practiced, even in the higher grades.

The first strand is Reading. Reading is broken into two parts: Informational and Literature. They both have four concepts (Key Ideas and Details, Craft and Structure, Integration of Knowledge and Ideas, and Range of Reading and Text Complexity) and ten standards, which are very similar; however, there are a few differences.

The second strand is Writing. Writing also has four concepts (Text Types and Purposes, Production and Distribution of Writing, Research to Build and Present Knowledge, and Range of Writing) and ten standards.

The third strand is Speaking and Listening. Speaking and Listening has two concepts (Comprehension and Collaboration and Presentation of Knowledge and Ideas) and six standards.

The final strand is Language. Language has three concepts (Conventions of Standard English, Knowledge of Language, and Vocabulary Acquisition and Use) and six standards. The CCSS also provide three appendices. Appendix A offers information on rigor and text complexity as well as an understanding of common language; appendix B offers text exemplar; and appendix C offers samples of student writing. For more information on understanding the CCSS, you can read *Pathways to the Common Core: Accelerating Achievement* by Lucy Calkins, Mary Ehrenworth, and Christopher Lehman (2012).

NARROWING THE LENS

To narrow the focus of this text even further, you will specifically discover how to help students interact with text multiple times by reading closely and purposefully to deepen comprehension of informational text.

Many of the strategies can be transferred or adapted for use with literary text (chapter 6 addresses this adaptation with literary text). You will discover where to start with reading closely and how to build rigor with texts and tasks. This focus helps move students toward mastery of all *CCR Anchor Standards for Reading Informational Texts*.

The reason for this shift is to help students meet the demands of a wide range of texts in college, career, and life. The CCSS guide students to increase their use of informational texts, as well as the amount of complex texts used for comprehension instruction. In addition, the CCSS emphasize reading text multiple times with different purposes, such as understanding explicit meaning, analyzing for structures, themes, and ideas, and evaluating arguments and claims in texts. Ultimately, it does not matter what standards you are teaching; these are simply good instructional practices that truly establish an environment for multiple interactions with text in order to challenge students' thinking, deepen their understanding, and build their intrinsic desire for lifelong learning.

This text will also open your curriculum and instruction to include multiliteracies (e.g., social media, advertisement, Internet, and environmental print), which the CCSS have included within the standards. Again, even without the CCSS, life requires students to interact with multiple forms of literacy critically in order to make well-informed decisions every day. Furthermore, the CCSS challenge students to use text evidence to support assertions made in writing or in responding to literal and critical questions. In other words, opinions are like rear ends; everyone has one and some are bigger than others, so people must support their opinions in order to have something to sit on.

KNOW-UNDERSTAND-DO ABOUT READING CLOSELY

CCR Anchor Standards for Reading state that students will be able to "*Read closely* to determine what the text says explicitly and to make logical inferences from it; cite specific textual evidence when writing or speaking to support conclusions drawn from the text" (p. 10). In addition, the CCSS (2010) state under the "Note on range and content of student reading," students will master " . . . reading independently and *closely*, which are essential to their future success" (p. 10).

Therefore, this approach to reading affords students an opportunity to master this type of reading. However, there has been debate that there is a difference between *Close and Careful Reading* and *Reading Closely*. Close and careful reading has been referenced when discussing literary analysis, whereas reading closely has been referenced for analyzing informational text.

Consequently, as more understanding of digging deeper into text surfaces, many educators and even researchers are beginning to use them synonymously. The main understanding for teachers is to know how to scaffold students' experiences with multiple literacies in order to allow for deeper understanding. The following are brief definitions of each, but the semantics of this discussion begs for further debate or discussion:

- *Close and Careful Reading for Literary Analysis* is the study of a work of fictional text that involves close and careful reading of certain sections in order to study the elements used and how the author unfolds events based on these elements.
- *Reading Closely to Deepen Understanding of Informational Text* addresses the 80 to 90 percent of what the CCSS in reading require—text-dependent analysis. The expectation for reading closely refers to questions teachers pose to students that should focus first on what a text says before you begin asking what it means and why it matters. This has nothing to do with how the reader feels about the text, nor what connections the reader can make with the text. The use of reading closely is to move from literal understanding to critical thinking about how and why the author made the decisions s/he did for the text being studied and the results of those choices on tone, purpose, and central idea.

So what is really being discussed here is students' need to interact with text multiple times for meaningful purposes in order to challenge their thinking, deepen their understanding, and build the desire for lifelong learning.

What do you need to *know* about reading closely? Reading closely is truly defined throughout the CCSS for Reading—specifically, within the first concept, *Key Ideas and Details*, as CCR Anchor Standard 1 defines what students will be able to do by the end of their school career. Students will be able to "read closely to determine what the text says explicitly and to make logical inferences from it; cite specific textual evidence when writing or speaking to support conclusions drawn from the text" (p. 35). However, it is also needed to be successful in life.

As a result, students must understand the topic, main idea, and supporting details in the text in order to use those details to read between the lines of the author's message after the cold read occurs. A *cold read* is the very first time a student is reading any given text. They have never seen the text before up to the moment it is placed in front of them, and zero background knowledge is built.

What do you need to *understand* about reading closely? Reading closely means diving back into the text for an expert read (reread) with a deeper purpose. An *expert read* is the second, third, or fourth time a student is reading any given text that they have experienced in the past. The text is not new to them, so they can use that familiarity to move from scratching the surface (literal meaning) to digging below the surface (critical meaning).

For example, CCR Anchor Standard 2 stretches students and says they will be able to "determine central ideas or themes of a text and analyze their development; summarize the key supporting details and ideas" (p. 35). This can come after processing time or after rereading complex text. In this standard, the word "analyze" brings attention to evaluating and studying text for deeper meaning, which can only be accomplished with complex text through multiple reading opportunities.

Reading closely is about rereading text with new perspectives in order to extract new information that may have gone unnoticed during the cold read. Think about a great book you have read several times. Did you gain something different each time? You most likely gathered a small detail that was overlooked the first time simply because during the first read you were grasping the basic understanding of the storyline. You can gain something new simply because you are in a different state of mind during your second read, or because of everything you experienced between the first read and the second read. Not sure this is true? Then pick up a book you have already read (maybe even from your high school years) and give it another read.

Professionally, you use reading closely throughout your day. You get an e-mail from your principal, and after the first read, you are not sure of implications, tone, or maybe even the literal meaning altogether. So you must go back and reread with a new lens. CCR Anchor Standard 3 has students do what good readers do every day in college and in careers in order to avoid misunderstandings and errors. Anchor Standard 3 states students will be able to "analyze how and why individuals, events, and ideas develop and interact over the course of a text" (p. 35). This forces students to think critically about how sentences build on one another and why the ideas are connected just as professionals do when they dissect an e-mail or a letter from a customer.

Critical readers do not just stop at the sentence level of understanding. Reading closely will lead students to break text apart at the word choice level. Students can think about why certain words are used and how the word choice changes the tone, bias, purpose, and perspective of the text. This technique is used every day in advertisement. For example, commercials for buying a permanent residence sell you on a home, not a house. Why? Mathematicians in particular need to reread in order to pay close attention to every word and how the words work together to elicit meaning, which leads to problem analysis and critical thinking.

Therefore, the second concept, *Craft and Structure*, has students go deeper into the text by peeling away at each layer. CCR Anchor Standard 4 addresses this level of analysis. Students will be able to "interpret words and phrases as they are used in a text, including determining technical, connotative, and figurative meanings, and analyze how specific word choices shape meaning or tone" (p. 35). This is a life skill in communication as well.

Connect this to how people use words when they communicate (irony, sarcasm, situational meaning [connotation versus denotation], and analogies) to make a point at work or express frustration. Think about advertisements; word choice is extremely important, say for example when selling an older vehicle. Dealers have switched from "used cars" to "previously owned cars." They did this because it changes the interpretation the reader may gather.

When you are trying to learn something new, fix an object that has broken, or discover how a piece of equipment works, you usually start with understanding the basics. Then you move to knowing the big picture or the whole piece. Next you break it apart piece by piece. Each step forces you to go a little deeper.

Finally, you bring it all back together to consider how it all works as a whole. CCR Anchor Standard 5 brings students back to the entire text.

Students will be able to "analyze the structure of texts, including how specific sentences, paragraphs, and larger portions of the text (e.g., a section, chapter, scene, or stanza) relate to each other and the whole" (p. 35). Text structure asks students to understand patterns, such as compare and contrast, cause and effect, time or process order, enumeration (listing), and classification.

When students understand and can identify the structure of the text, then they can begin to understand the author's purpose or perspective for writing the text. So CCR Anchor Standard 5 directly impacts CCR Anchor Standard 6, as students will be able to "assess how point of view or purpose shapes the content and style of a text" (p. 35). This leads to evaluating the information as fact or opinion, which leads to further inquiry in order to triangulate the key information presented. Ultimately, this will prepare them for argument to support claims.

Once students have torn one piece of text apart, they can begin to use the same process on a wide range of text and media sources. Adults do this often when they are deciding whether to buy a product that claims to yield certain results, or when citizens are determining whom to vote for during elections. This type of wide-range reading and research through multiliteracy sources is exactly what CCR Anchor Standard 7 is asking students to be able to do, "integrate and evaluate content presented in diverse formats and media, including visually and quantitatively, as well as in words" (p. 35), which is why CCR Anchor Standard 7 falls under the third concept, *Integration of Knowledge and Ideas*. Students will ask questions and challenge information they see, hear, and read from multimedia literacies and then represent their challenges in multiple formats.

Once they can represent their thinking about the text graphically (numerically) or in some way to communicate to others, then they are ready to cross-examine and prove or negate those challenges. CCR Anchor Standard 8 under *Integration of Knowledge and Ideas* states students will be able to "delineate and evaluate the argument and specific claims in a text, including the validity of the reasoning as well as the relevance and sufficiency of the evidence" (p. 35). What a great opportunity to teach students about domains (.com, .org, .edu, .gov, etc.), as well as fallacies (circular reasoning, bandwagon, emotional appeal, etc.).

The last standard in the third concept forces students to use all the previous standards when examining two or more texts because they have to understand the literal meaning (standards 1–3). Then they have to tear the texts apart piece by piece to understand the critical meaning (standards 4–6). Finally they have to be able to cross-examine texts in the highest level of thinking to form new beliefs and opinions (standards 7–9) that will mold them into adults.

So CCR Anchor Standard 9 finalizes the transformation of knowledge, as students will be able to "analyze how two or more texts address similar themes or topics in order to build knowledge or to compare the approaches the authors take" (p. 35). Think about what this looks like in the real world. You get credit card offers in the mail and you need to determine which one is the best option. You want to move but you need to compare neighborhood statistics to ensure a safe and healthy environment for your family. You need to buy a new car but you need to compare and contrast make and model to cost and gas consumption. CCR Anchor Standard 9 works its way into many facets of adult life, so it is extremely important for students to master.

The final concept is *Range of Reading and Text Complexity*, which gives most educators a run for their money. It requires much knowledge to be in place before teachers can plan for deliberate practice. A range of reading means students will explore several genres, as well as multi-literacies, such as social media and advertisements focused on a subject or topic. This means students will gain knowledge from reading several pieces of texts, not just the textbook. Finally, you need to consider different levels of text complexity, which requires a knowledge of the components (qualitative, quantitative, and reader and task).

IMPLICATIONS

Accordingly, CCR Anchor Standard 10 defines that all students will "read and comprehend complex literary and informational texts independently and proficiently" (p. 35). This standard leads to implications for teachers. They will have to go beyond the approved textbook to provide students exposure and experience with multiple literacies presenting information about their content. Teachers will have to hold students accountable for discussion and writing to sources about their content.

So, the other major implication is teachers need to be able to choose grade level text and scaffold learning around that text so that all students are able to digest the information and process the key ideas. As students progress, the text should become more challenging. This means the content becomes more focused, demanding, and specific; the sentence structure varies in length, and vocabulary is content (or domain) specific; and the tasks become more rigorous (*Webb's Depth of Knowledge, Bloom's taxonomy,* or *Marzano's taxonomy*). For more in-depth information on rigor and text complexity, you can read *Text Complexity: Raising Rigor in Reading* by Douglas Fisher, Nancy Frey, and Diane Lapp (2012).

Planning backward for each of these standards or a combination of these standards, with a wide range of texts and tasks, is not an easy undertaking to accomplish. It requires you to identify what students need to know, understand, and do in order to demonstrate mastery of skills defined throughout the standards. More importantly, planning for this type of reading requires you, the teacher, to practice and master this type of text interaction first and foremost before you can even teach your students to read closely. "For our students to read this way, we need to read this way" (Calkins, Ehrenworth, & Lehman, 2012, p. 88).

FINAL THOUGHT

This professional text will walk you through three different approaches to help students read closely. These are not the only ways students can read closely, but they are options to get you started. This is not a program; they are strategies to help students have multiple interactions with a wide range of literacies. Reading closely is a way good readers approach complex texts with several layers to move from literal understanding of text to critical understanding of text, and triangulate sources in order to validate or negate thinking.

In the following chapters, you will discover three ways to help your students interact with text multiple times. Each way challenges the students to go deeper and think critically about nonfiction text in every class. Figure 1.1 provides you with an overview of each of the ways to read closely. These strategies do not tell students what to think but empower

Overview of Reading Closely & Writing Purposefully Options

	1st Interaction with Text:	2nd Interaction with Text:	3rd Interaction with Text:	4th Interaction with Text:
	Set purpose and cold read to build explicit understanding of text.	Conduct an expert read with a new purpose to deepen text understanding of the implicit meaning.	Refer to the text to cite evidence to support discussion, questions, and responses.	Analyze the word choice and sentence/paragraph relationships against explicit and implicit meaning.
Change Perspective	Teacher introduces standard(s) and sets know, understand and do (KUD). And builds brief background knowledge/vocabulary. Student engages in cold, independent read of text. Ask what is the topic and what does the author want you to know about the topic?	Teacher establishes a new purpose for expert read generated by proving a question, skill or persona. Students generate and share out evidence to support their role.	Teacher models answering questions aligned to different taxonomies using text evidence to validate responses. Students will practice through gradual release.	Students focus on word choice (semantics) to determine point of view/bias/ tone/purpose in relationship to central ideas across multiple literacies in order to be critical readers. Students will practice through GRR
Preview/ Review	Teacher introduces standard(s), KUD. & builds vocabulary knowledge. Students engage in preview process and cold read of text. Ask what is the topic and what does the author want you to know about the topic?	Teacher sets a new focus for expert read by asking students to create a table of contents in the margins. Students engage in a cold read and summarize each paragraph in 5 words or less in the margins.	Teacher models answering questions aligned to different taxonomies using text evidence guided by table of contents to validate responses. Students will practice through gradual release.	Students focus on word choice (semantics) to determine point of view/bias/ tone/purpose in relationship to central ideas across multiple literacies in order to be critical readers. Students will practice through GRR
Strategic Approach	Teacher presents a LO in the form of an activator question for students to discuss. Then brainstorm possible reasons. Teacher build vocabulary. Students engage in "Cold Read" and revisit brainstorm and possible reasons.	Teacher sets TSM purpose for expert read, allows time for students to process text together, and provide why. Students engage in expert reading text coding text structures.	Teachers has students read a 3rd time with CTS & text evidence support discussion. Students engage in CTS & text evidence support discussion, & writing to demonstrate learning.	Students focus on word choice (semantics) to determine point of view/bias/ tone/purpose in relationship to central ideas across multiple literacies in order to be critical readers. Students will practice through GRR

Key: CCSS = common core state standards; KUD = know, understand, do; BR = before reading; LO = learning objective; TSM= test structure marking; CTS= categorize text structure

Figure 1.1. Reading Closely & Writing Purposefully Overview

them on how to think critically through the gradual release of responsibility (GRR) process.

You will also discover how to walk students back through a text multiple times in order to examine word choice, sentence structure and relationships, and distinguish presented information as fact or opinion. This text will conclude with helping you connect these strategies to other genres as well as other forms of literacies (e.g., Internet, social media, advertisements, etc.). So what are you waiting for? Turn the page and start reading, but do not be afraid to reread—in fact, multiple interactions with each chapter are highly encouraged. After all, this is reading closely!

Chapter Two

Open the Mind with Change Perspective

A Reading Closely Approach

A science teacher from a high school arrives at a biology training a few minutes early. He heads over to the presenter to say hi and see how his colleague is doing. Somewhere in the conversation, they start discussing what the teacher managed to get through during the first half of the year. "Well, I only made it to chapter 3 because most of my students failed the first couple of tests, so I had to go back and review what I already taught. I realize the pacing guide says I should be in chapter 4, but that's an easier chapter, so I can make up time there and catch up," Mr. Strum explains.

This response is pretty typical when you ask teachers what they are teaching. Big ideas, key concepts, and textbook chapters—most teachers have a general idea of what should be taught based on those curriculum pieces, but how well do you know your standards?

Instead of planning from textbooks or around curriculum resources, think about these questions. Do you know and understand every word of your standards? Do you have a clear way to assess or measure whether students are able to demonstrate mastery of your standards? Can you provide examples of what students need to know, understand, and do in order to demonstrate mastery of the standard(s) by the end of the lesson, unit, quarter, or school year? Are you aware of how to build on knowledge in order to scaffold learning? What will you do if students do not respond in the way you intend?

Each of these considerations leads to intentional planning—planning with the end in mind, which then allows you to choose the best instructional practices and strategies to truly move students toward mastery of your content. Intentional planning is not something that can be done quickly in one planning period, nor is it something that should be accomplished in isolation, but with a team of teachers collaborating over time. This approach to planning is key for guiding students through reading closely with texts because it guides you to think critically about the text you select and exactly what you need or want students to take away from it in order to move toward content mastery.

Whether you are an English/language arts (ELA) teacher, reading teacher, history teacher, or science teacher, you must embed ELA standards. No, you are not a reading teacher, but you are a teacher of your discipline, which means students need direct, facilitated, and differentiated instruction to attack texts in your class utilizing ELA standards, which are ultimately life skills.

Therefore, you need to help students understand how to read for explicit meaning, identify central ideas, and connect the details together. You need to help students use discipline-specific vocabulary (technical meaning), use structures to analyze ideas, and explain how the point of view or purpose of the text conveys meaning and tone. You need to integrate multimedia sources, guide students through evaluating multiple sources, as well as compare and contrast those sources. All of this is done through the use of a wide range of text (primary and secondary sources) at various levels of complexity to ensure all students deepen their understanding of your discipline through multiple interactions with a critical lens.

So if you agree with these expectations, then you are helping students reach grade level mastery of the *Common Core State Standards for English/Language Arts and Literacy in History/Social Studies, Science, and Technical Subjects* or the ability to thrive in life and not just survive.

Embedding ELA standards is not easily accomplished without intentional planning. First, you start by selecting your discipline-specific standard(s) you need to teach. For example, you teach sixth grade science, and you are currently instructing students on the big idea *Organization and Development of Living Organisms*.

For the purpose of this example, you will focus your curriculum and instructional decisions around the standard, students will be able to "compare and contrast types of infectious agents that may infect the human body, including viruses, bacteria, fungi, and parasites" (CPALMS, 2012, SC.6.L.14.6). Then you decide how you will measure whether students know, understand, and can apply the standard(s). Also, you need to think about checking for understanding along the way by using formative assessment. One such way is using a ticket out the door or Poll Everywhere (www.polleverywhere.com/).

Next, determine what text you will use and what you will do to move students toward mastery. If you choose to activate knowledge and spark interest first, then you may choose high interest grade level texts, such as "Bacteria: The Good, the Bad, and the Stinky" by Joy Masoff in *Read-Aloud Anthology* by Janet Allen and Patrick Daley (2004) and/or an excerpt from *The Demon in the Freezer* by Richard Preston (2002).

Once you choose what text you will use, think about what students need to get out of the text. How deep do they need to go? How difficult is the text in terms of discipline-specific vocabulary (tier 3 words, technical meaning, content terms), sentence structure (long or short), and big ideas or concepts? What do you want students to do with the text? Each of these questions addresses text complexity. For more information on text complexity, you can read *Text Complexity: Raising Rigor in Reading* by Nancy Frey, Diane Lapp, and Douglas Fisher (2012). For a quantitative measure on text, you can visit Source Rater at http://naeptba.ets.org/SourceRater3/.

This intentional planning will naturally lead you to decide how you will use the text(s) as well as ways you will help students interact with the text(s). In this chapter, you will learn how to use the gradual release instructional framework with a reading closely strategy in order for students to develop an interest and understanding about infectious agents. The standard mentioned earlier will be broken into a four-week unit of instruction with four learning targets (bacteria, viruses, fungi, and parasites). The summative assessment will require students to write a compare and contrast paper on infectious agents using evidence from texts, videos, pictures, labs, and literary texts to support their analysis.

So, let's get started. The first strategy is called *Change Perspective*. It does not matter what you call the approaches for reading closely, rather that you understand how to intentionally plan so that students will interact with text multiple times in order to promote lifelong learning and a deeper understanding of complex texts.

PLANNING FOR CHANGE PERSPECTIVE

In this section you learn how to plan for change perspective, the first approach to reading closely, which helps students understand there are different ways to look at the world around them in order to validate or invalidate information or agree or disagree with information, you will be introduced to the overall structure of this approach, then the planning process, and finally the teaching process.

This reading closely approach addresses perspective and point of view (Common Core State Standard for Reading Informational Text 1 and 6, RI.6-12.1 and RI.6-12.6). This approach challenges students to interact with text three to four different times to view it and interpret it from several directions of thinking.

The first step in planning is to create a learning objective, decide if there is any background knowledge and/or vocabulary knowledge that will need to be briefly discussed prior to reading, and finally read the text one time through. In the second interaction with the text, the teacher sets a new purpose for reading, connected to the learning objective required for students to look at the text differently in order to collect specific evidence during a second read of the entire text. Promote an atmosphere that allows students time to share identified evidence and implications with a partner and with the entire class.

For a third interaction with the text, the teacher models text-dependent questions and then has students work with a partner to practice text-dependent questions. Always bring the class back together to gauge their level of practice and validate thinking. If you choose to venture into a fourth interaction with the text, then you will plan for students to analyze the word level, which will lead students to evaluate the craft and structure (purpose, tone, perspective, point of view, etc.), as well as the integration of knowledge and ideas (text structures, word analysis, relationships, etc.). This is further explained in chapter 5 and is represented in the last column of the reading closely overview shared in chapter 1, figure 1.1.

As you read through this instructional approach, change perspective, refer back to the sixth grade science standard mentioned earlier—students will be able to "compare and contrast types of infectious agents that may infect the human body, including viruses, bacteria, fungi, and parasites" (CPALMS, 2012, SC.6.L.14.6). As an example, this four-week unit will start with using the two texts mentioned earlier—"Bacteria: The Good, the Bad, and the Stinky" by Joy Masoff in *Read-Aloud Anthology* by Janet Allen and Patrick Daley (2004), and an excerpt from *The Demon in the Freezer* by Richard Preston (2002), in addition to a third text, *The Black Death, 1348* (2001) from www.eyewitnesstohistory.com as well as the textbook, videos, and novels.

Remember the creativity of teaching is making instructional decisions that truly inspire learning. Choose additional texts in order to set the stage for students to cross analyze and build knowledge from a diverse group of sources on all four parts of the standard (bacteria, viruses, fungi, and parasites). These texts are great activators to get the students interested in learning about science.

Think about how you can adapt this approach, not adopt. You can use an article and then explore pieces of the textbook and repeat the process. The purpose is for students to learn how to open their minds to multiple ways of looking at any given text, truly understand the literal meaning of the text, and dig deeper by dissecting the text in multiple ways.

Now that you have a big picture understanding of what change perspective looks like, you are ready to start the planning process for reading closely to learn content-specific information. You will find a template to guide you through planning for change perspective, the first reading closely approach, in appendix A.

When you choose the text, you must read the text. Too often teachers read assigned text for the first time with the students. This cannot happen, because it does not allow teachers to intentionally plan for intentional teaching of difficult concepts or vocabulary, higher-order discussion, and the facilitation of meaningful and deep reading connections to the learning objective. Whatever you plan to have your students do with the text, you must do first (prior to entering the classroom). By reading the text ahead of time, you will be able to ensure it is content appropriate for your students as well as ensure the text truly lends itself to teaching the big idea or concepts you believe it will teach to help move students toward mastery of the standard(s).

Go ahead and pull your text. The text for this example is "Bacteria: The Good, the Bad, and the Stinky" by Joy Masoff in *Read-Aloud Anthology* by Janet Allen and Patrick Daley (2004). First number each paragraph. Then set a timer while you read the text through (word for word) the first time. If you are a fast reader, then you need to plan for students to require three times your clock. If you are a slower reader, then you need to plan for students to require two times your clock. For example, if you read this text in six minutes and seventeen seconds, then consider your students and give them seven to twelve minutes for an initial read.

The first read should be for familiarity for you during lesson planning and for the students during the lesson. From this point forward, the first read will be referred to as the "cold" read. The first reading standard for grades 6 through 12 states students will be able to "read closely to determine what the text says explicitly" (College and Career Readiness Anchor Standards for Reading, p. 35), so you need to ensure a literal understanding of the text (who, what, when, and where).

During your cold read, circle words you anticipate students might have difficulty with during their interaction with the text. This will allow you to front-load key vocabulary prior to reading in order to increase comprehension, or you can plan a mini activity for students to work with the key words, such as word splash, prior to reading. For more ideas about vocabulary, you can read *Words Their Way with Struggling Readers: Word Study for Reading, Vocabulary, and Spelling Instruction, Grades 4-12* by Kevin Flanigan, Latisha Hayes, Shane Templeton, and Donald Bear (2010). Background knowledge can be built or discussed based on what has been read or learned so far; for example, you can introduce a lesson with a quality picture book or a quick video clip or with a few words that can spark discussion around predictions. Front-loading information should be brief and take less than five minutes of your class time.

Now, ask yourself, "What is important for students to know about this text, understand about this text, and do with the information from this text based on your content-specific grade level standard(s)?" This will help you create your learning objective, and it will help you decide which ELA standards you will need to embed for the interaction with the text to be more beneficial. If you are a reading or language arts teacher, then you start with the ELA standard, choose your topic/theme, select your text, and then choose your instructional practice and strategy.

Then during your planning process, read the text(s) a second time. This time as you read, think about two different ways (perspectives) to interact with the text. The reason for this dual approach to reading is to stimulate discussion among students that will require them to cite evidence from the text to support their perspective, which gets them ready for argumentative writing and debates. As a result, students will be able "to make logical inferences from it; cite specific textual evidence when writing or speaking to support conclusions drawn from the text" (College and Career Readiness Anchor Standards for Reading, p. 35). From this point forward in the text, the second read will be referred to as an "expert" read. By using different words other than reread, students who struggle are more likely to willingly participate.

For example, you may have a text that lends itself well for half the class to read for causes and the other half to read for effects. Another approach that students may be able to do during an expert read is partner A reads for facts and partner B reads for opinions. Table 2.1 offers several ways to change perspectives during an expert read.

The perspective or purpose you establish for the expert read should be connected to your grade level standards, move students toward an understanding of the learning objective, and provide students a reason to move from a literal understanding of text to a critical understanding of text. The set perspectives will determine which concept students are reading to work toward.

You do not always need to have two perspectives for the expert read. You may have only one perspective or use a driving question that students read to identify evidence in the text to support their answer(s) or position(s) they may have about the topic (an example of this way is provided in chapter 6). The most important thing to remember is to challenge students to look at the text with a new lens, different from their current belief or thinking. If you have students open their minds, then they will be better equipped to solve problems that arise in the real world rather than feel trapped in a corner with no way out during difficult times.

Table 2.1. Optional Reading Closely Perspectives for Informational Text

Perspective A	Perspective B
Problem	Solution
Comparison	Contrast
Good/Right	Evil/Wrong
Soldier	Civilian
Active	Passive
Threat	Hope
Cause	Effect
Fact	Opinion
Ruler	Subject
Communist	Capitalist
Activist	Conservative
Protector	Eradicator
Optimist	Pessimist
Realist	Idealist
Supporter	Detractor
Detective/Investigator	Reporter

For example, students may read to "assess how point of view or purpose shapes the content and style of a text" (College and Career Readiness Anchor Standards for Reading, p. 35). Partner A reads for author's point of view using identifiers (signal words), such as *I, you,* or *they,* and partner B reads for author's purpose using identifiers, such as *numbers, should, must, humor.*

The discussion that follows has students analyze how point of view and purpose work together to shape the meaning or message of the text, citing to be right. For instance, in the text mentioned earlier, "Bacteria: The Good, the Bad, and the Stinky" by Joy Masoff in *Read-Aloud Anthology* by Janet Allen and Patrick Daley (2004), have partner A read to highlight all information supporting the use of bacteria for good and have partner B read to highlight all information supporting the use of bacteria for evil. This is directly connected back to the standard also mentioned earlier, students will be able to "compare and contrast types of infectious agents that may infect the human body, including viruses, bacteria, fungi, and parasites" (CPALMS, 2012, SC.6.L.14.6).

Once you determine the purpose for the expert read and determine it will work, develop a range of questions using Webb's Depth of Knowledge, Bloom's taxonomy, or Marzano's taxonomy as a guide. It is important to create questions prior to teaching with the text(s) because it is difficult to come up with higher-order questions on the spot. There are four levels of questions.

The first level, which is the lowest cognitive level, has students simply identify or locate information in the text, such as who, what, when, where (i.e., topic, main idea, details). Level 2 questions require the student to read between the lines—use the information the text supplies, as well as prior knowledge, such as infer, interpret, distinguish, or predict. The third level of questions requires the students to go beyond the words of the text, but use the text to spark out-of-the-box thinking, such as assess, revise, formulate. Level 4 questions, the highest level of cognitive complexity, ask the students to design, apply, create, prove based on what they have learned in reading, research, and life.

In addition, teach students how to be text dependent when they answer all types of questions. You should think about how to model this type of response to questions. This is a step you want to ensure happens! Modeling how to think through different types of questions, go back into the text to cite to be right, and triangulate information is very important.

Using the text as a support helps students move from understanding key ideas and details to integration of knowledge and ideas. Again this must be purposefully planned. Once students have worked through questioning and citing evidence to support their responses, always give them time to process those choices with a partner or in small groups. You can follow this with a whole-class share out in order to gauge their understanding and discussion.

Finally, think about how you will check for understanding at the end of the lesson. This is important because it will drive what you choose to do with the class on the following instructional days. A check for understanding can be done in many different ways; for example, a ticket out the door that states the learning objective in the form of a question. Another quick way to check for understanding is to use technology, such as have students use their cell phones to text responses while Poll Everywhere (www.polleverywhere.com) collects and graphs the incoming data in real time.

In the next section of this chapter, you will read about how this lesson unfolds in a sixth grade classroom. Appendix B offers additional lesson plans for intermediate, middle school, and high school.

TEACHING CHANGE PERSPECTIVE

Consider the following scenario of a sixth grade teacher who uses reading closely, change perspective approach, with the article "Bacteria: The Good, the Bad, and the Stinky" by Joy Masoff in *Read-Aloud Anthology* by Janet Allen and Patrick Daley (2004). Watch how she gradually releases the responsibility to the students throughout the lesson. The lesson can take anywhere from forty-five to sixty minutes depending on your students, how comfortable you are with the approach, how long the text is, and how much "teacher talk" occurs. You can also break the steps up into different days.

The late bell rings and students quickly rush to their seats and fumble through their book bags. Students are in several different places with their willingness and readiness to get to work. Some have their learning logs out and are copying down the learning objective, "Students will be able to identify and explain the differences between good and bad bacteria." Others are writing in their planners the day's agenda and homework. A few are just sitting back and simply waiting for something amazing to happen, or waiting for the last minute of the class to tick away.

The teacher closes the door behind her and greets the class, "All right . . . all right . . . let's get started, everyone. I see some of you are ready to open your minds and learn something new today. If you're not ready, let's change your path now." A few groans echo across the room, but the students prepare for the day's lesson.

"I'm going to help you learn a new reading approach today. It's an important one because it will help you to view texts from more than one perspective. When you can look at anything from multiple perspectives, then you are able to help yourself problem-solve, seek solutions, and get out of sticky situations. How many of you have an opinion?" Every single hand shoots up!

"Great!" Ms. Williams says as she glances at all the hands. "Well, opinions are like rear ends; everyone has one, and some are bigger than others, so we must learn to support them." Laughter erupts from the mouth of every student. "Good. I have your attention. When we state an opinion or answer, we must learn to provide evidence or support as to why our opinion or answer is the best."

"By the end of class today, I want you to be able to use evidence to support your answer to the learning object, identify and explain the differences between good and bad bacteria. You will be able to do this by reading an article, 'Bacteria: The Good, the Bad, and the Stinky' by Joy Masoff, and using the approach I'll teach you today. Are there any questions about how we'll spend our learning time today?" Ms. Williams asks. Students look around, but no one raises his/her hand.

"I want to bring your attention to a few words you may struggle with when you read this text, and I don't want you to get caught up on words. I want you to focus on the text and the approach that will help you deepen your understanding of the text," Ms. Williams explains as she passes out the article.

Ms. Williams places a text for herself under the document projector and directs students, "After you write your name and date on the top, number each paragraph like I'm doing."

The teacher finishes numbering her paragraphs, looks up to see students finishing, and says, "Thumbs up if you also numbered twelve paragraphs. Excellent. By numbering our paragraphs, we'll be able to reference specific places in the text to support our discussion later."

"Put your finger on paragraph 1. In the last sentence, you will see the word *monera.* Circle that word. When you are reading and you come to this word, you'll be able to refer to the vocabulary chart at the front of the room, or you can write the brief definition next to the word in the margin, like I'm going to do. This word means a group of organisms," Ms. Williams explains.

"It sounds like Panera," Alex shouts out. The teacher grins and shakes her head at the connection.

"Put your finger on paragraph 4. In the first sentence, find and circle the word *microorganisms*. I see a prefix I know," Ms. Williams prompts.

"Oh, yeah—micro," Jenna says.

"That means small," Josh pipes into the conversation.

"Aren't organisms like bacteria?" Melissa asks.

"That's an example of an organism, but an organism is any creature or system defined by functions. Good discussion. Do you have any other thoughts about this word?" No one chimes in, so she continues. "Okay, so put your finger on paragraph 8. In the second sentence, the word *Salmonella* and . . . " the teacher begins.

"That's the fish!" Jessica yells out with excitement.

"Well, Jess, I see a similarity in the word, but notice this is different than salmon," the teacher records on the whiteboard. "*Salmonella* is a bacterium that causes food poisoning. Now look at paragraph 9, last sentence. Circle the word *Legionnaires' disease*. This is a type of pneumonia caused by a bacterium."

"Ms. Williams, what's bacterium?" Jessica asks.

"Bacterium is the singular for bacteria. All right, last one. Go to paragraph 10, last sentence. Circle *acidophilus*, which means bacteria used to make yogurt and probiotics. These are good bacteria taken after medication kills all the bacteria in order to restore your system back to full health. Are there any questions about these words?" Ms. Williams inquires.

"Okay. I'm going to give you six minutes to do your cold read. Remember it's a cold read because we've never read this text before, just like you jump into the pool without checking the temperature. So you can't have anything in your hands to write on the text. When you're done, I also want you to remember that we're a family who quietly sits and waits for all members to finish reading so we don't distract those who may need the entire time. Raise your hand if you remember the vow of silence you took during reading time. Great! I'll be walking around if you need coaching to crash through the text. Are you ready?" the teacher asks. Students shake their heads up and down. "Let's cold read!"

During the cold read, Ms. Williams moves around the class, watching students' fingers and eyes move through the text. She also watches for signs of frustration, such as slouched body, wrinkled foreheads, hands rubbing faces or heads, so she can provide immediate coaching for students in these situations in order to quickly and successfully help them adjust their approach before the trigger leads to total shutdown.

"Class, time's up and I see everyone's finished. Now think for a minute—what is the topic of the text and what does the author want you to know about that topic?"

Ms. Williams writes on the board an equation (topic + what the author wants you to know = main idea). "Now turn to your shoulder partner. The partner whose birthday is closest to January will share first—what's the topic, and the other partner will listen. Then switch roles and the partner who listened will now share—what the author wants you to know about that topic. Go!" Ms. Williams sets them loose and walks around to quickly listen to each pair's discussion. She gets to her readers who struggle first to ensure they get it.

"The text is about bacteria," Lashonda shares with her partner Jeff.

"Not just bacteria, but good and bad bacteria," Jeff adds.

"Oh, well yeah, that's what I meant," Lashonda clarifies.

"The author wants you to know that there are bacteria that aren't good for you and will make you sick, and that there are bacteria that are good for you that'll help you," Josh shares with Kathryn.

"This is gross. I'm gonna make sure I always wash my hands," Kathryn points out.

"Okay, class. I heard some great discussion. Let's fill out our investigation reports. Who is this text about?" Ms. Williams poses.

"Bacteria," all the students shout out at once.

"How do you know?" Ms. Williams challenges. "Jessica?"

"Well, because it's the word that repeats over and over again throughout the text," Jessica answers.

"Good. Now what does the author want you to know about the topic?" Ms. Williams questions.

"Okay, so there are good bacteria and there are bad bacteria," Alvino shares.

"How do you know that?" Ms. Williams wonders.

"Because every paragraph either talks about something good or something bad," Alvino states.

"No! There's stinky too," Lashonda yells out.

"Is that good or bad?" Ms. Williams inquires.

"I think bad cause when something smells, you don't wanna be near it," Lashonda explains.

"Okay. When can you find bacteria?" Ms. Williams asks.

"Anytime!" the class yells out.

"How do you know this?" Ms. Williams inquires. "Melissa?"

"There's not like a date listed, but the way the author tells you all the places you can find bacteria, I guess that it means you can also find them at any time. You know . . . anywhere," Melissa explains.

"Well, Melissa, you also answered my next question, which is where can you find bacteria?" the teacher says. "So who can use the text to support Melissa's opinion that bacteria can be found anywhere?"

"I'll do it, Ms. Williams," Jeff speaks up. "In paragraph 1, sentence 2, the author states that bacteria can be found in dirt and in the ocean. Then paragraph 3, sentence 3, states they can be found on your skin cause they love the oil. You want me to keep going?"

"Have we uncovered enough evidence to cite to be right?" Ms. Williams answers.

"Okay, I like this next part cause the text says bacteria is in your poop, so that's every human, probably every day," Jeff adds while other students express their disgust with that piece of the text.

"Excellent discussion with evidence from the text in order to cite to be right. Now, let's open our minds and explore this text differently. We will participate in an expert read. This means you have already read the text once and are familiar with the basic understanding of the text. So we will explore it again with a different purpose in order to deepen our understanding and work toward truly demonstrating our knowledge of the learning objective. The partner whose birthday is closest to January will be a mad scientist looking for evidence in the text to use bacteria to take over the world; you will use a purple highlighter to tag your text evidence. The other partner will be a good scientist looking for evidence in the text to use bacteria to help mankind and will use a blue highlighter to tag text evidence. Let me show you what this looks like," Ms. Williams explains.

28 Chapter Two

"If you are the mad scientist, hold up your purple highlighter," the teacher directs half the class. "Everyone put your finger next to paragraph 1. You follow along as I read out loud. *Bacteria are tiny . . . ,*" Ms. Williams begins. As she continues to read, she stops after sentence 3. "I noticed that sentence 2 and 3 tell me where I can find bacteria and how they thrive, so I'm going to highlight both of those sentences because as a mad scientist, I'm able to go and collect the bacteria and then set up the environment it'll thrive in so I can take over the world," Ms. Williams elaborates. "Yes, Lashonda?"

"Okay, so I'm a good scientist and I'd be interested in that information, but for where I can collect it in order to study how it thrives so I can discover how to destroy it, right?" Lashonda sort of states and asks. Other good scientists echo her opinion.

"Lashonda, this is not about being right or wrong. This is about supporting the reason for tagging the evidence in the text, which you did. Way to go!" Ms. Williams clarifies. "Before you start your expert read, make a key, like this (see figure 2.1 for Ms. Williams's key), at the top of your paper, so I know which perspective you read from when I collect this at the end of class. I believe we're clear on our purpose for our expert read. You're reading with a new perspective, which you'll share and support with your partner after six minutes. Are there any questions?"

Students are ready and willing to reread this text because they are excited about the perspectives chosen in order to answer the learning objective—identify and explain the differences between good and bad

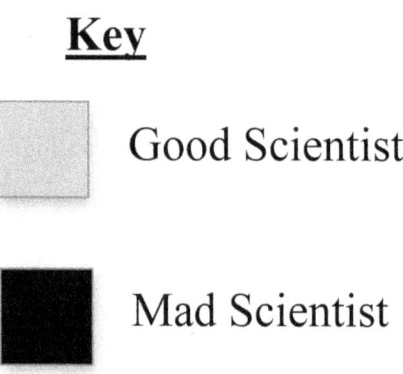

Figure 2.1. Change Perspective Sample Key

bacteria. "Let's expert read, then," Ms. Williams instructs after waiting for any questions.

While the students participate in the expert read, Ms. Williams is walking around to make sure students understand the task. Occasionally she stops to ask why a student has highlighted but only to ensure they get the purpose. By walking around while students interact with text, she sends a clear message about the importance of this task!

After six minutes, she stops the class. "I see we're all done with our expert read. I want you to turn to your partners. Good scientists, you will have one minute to share what you tagged and why, then I will ask you to switch and mad scientists will share what they tagged and why. After two minutes, we will share out our favorite piece of evidence and why with the entire class," Ms. Williams explains. "Alvino, will you restate the directions I just gave in middle school language so your peers can understand better?"

"So I'm gonna tell my partner what I highlighted in blue as the good scientist and why I think it's important and then when you say to, Melissa's gonna tell me what she highlighted in purple as the mad scientist and why she thinks it's important. Then we need to be ready to tell you what we talked about, that it?" Alvino says.

"You got it. Ready, experts? Let's talk with our partners," Ms. Williams directs. As students share, the teacher moves around the class to listen to their evidence and support. She is prepared to redirect if she needs to, but every students seems to be following the directions. "Switch!" The mad scientists really got into it as they shared about using bacteria to take over the world.

"Time! Let's hear what you've come up with, scientists," Ms. Williams challenges. "Josh."

"So as a mad scientist, I highlighted evidence in paragraph 6, sentence 1, because once I find bacteria, I'm gonna throw a huge party and infect the food with lots of bacteria and everyone will get all kinds of sick," Josh excitedly shares. While he shares this information, Ms. Williams records his evidence and support on a T-chart (see table 2.2).

"You've really thought this through, Josh. Should I be worried?" Ms. Williams inquires with a smile. Josh shakes his head from side to side, laughing. "What about an example of what a good scientist would want to know and why? Kathy."

Table 2.2. Evidence for Change Perspective Sample Lesson

Good Scientist	Mad Scientist
"... bacteria help break down animal hides ..." (para. 4, sent. 5)	"... causing food poisoning, strep throat, pneumonia, diarrhea ..." (para. 6, sent. 1)
"... used to make vaccines, medicines, yogurt, and even tea!" (para. 4, sent. 6)	"... bacteria are spread is through bad hygiene." (para. 7, sent. 1)

"Okay . . . in paragraph 4, last sentence. I can know how to make good bacteria for people to eat, like in yogurt, in order to help fight off the bad bacteria. This is important because as people get sick, I can help them feel better. You know, like attack the bad bacteria in their body that Josh is gonna cause," Kathy shares with a smirk.

"Both excellent examples of good and bad uses of bacteria. I've captured both of those pieces of evidence on our T-chart, which we can use to help us answer and support questions. Let me show you how this is done," suggests the teacher. "How does understanding bacteria help the human body?

Good scientists have already highlighted this evidence. As a good reader, I'll think about what I highlighted as good uses of bacteria. Then I'll read each option to see if I can eliminate any choices. In this case, I can cross out letter *D* because the article didn't mention the use of bacteria to *help* you poop. Now I'll skim through my highlighted portions and notice paragraphs 4, 7, and 10 all provide evidence to support letter *C* as the best option. Okay, now you try. With your shoulder partner find the evidence in the text that supports your answer to the question *What is the author's purpose for writing this text?* Be prepared to explain why," Ms. Williams explains.

Ms. Williams gives the students three minutes to discuss the question, agree on an answer, and find evidence in the text that supports their decision. "Eyes on me," she calls for their attention. "On your whiteboards, partner A write the letter choice and partner B write the location of support." The teacher scans the classroom and notices all the students have the correct answer and evidence.

"Erase your whiteboards and put them off to the side. I'm going to give you each a sticky note, and I want you to use your text to independently answer this question: Explain the differences between good and bad bacteria and how they impact human life. Remember to use evidence to support your opinion. Pack up when you're done," Ms. Williams directs the students.

After a few minutes, the students are asked to pack up if they have not already done so. When the bell rings, the students stand and walk out the door, handing their sticky note to the teacher.

FINAL THOUGHT

It is not enough to simply accept an answer or an opinion from students. Teachers must challenge students to view texts and situations from multiple perspectives. This reading closely approach does just that. It forces students to see text with a new mind-set or focus; it opens their minds. Teachers must also question students with why. This also forces students to really think about why they believe or think something instead of just simply making random comments: an open mind that thinks before it speaks and responds instead of reacts, which means students are more likely to avoid predicaments or be able to solve problems. How will you change your students' perspective and challenge their minds?

Chapter Three

Actively Read with Preview/Review

Active reading seems to be an unnatural action for students. There are several reasons this is true. It never fails—you hand students a text to read with a few questions, and the first thing students do is read the questions and skim for answers. They are not reading to learn or gather the author's big idea(s); they are reading to get done. It is a race to the finish.

Another crime against reading that often occurs in classes is the teacher holds all knowledge and simply acts as the deliverer of this knowledge, and the students spend very little time reading anything. Part of the problem is students must spend time reading in each and every class in order to continue to refine and improve this process. You already know this subject; you have a degree in it, but your students do not, so let them experience it through reading, writing, and discussion. You will be amazed at how much more engagement and learning takes place when you simply coach, and students do all the work. Reading text multiple times will help with this instructional process.

Students do not understand that good readers read texts multiple times for deeper understanding, connections, and distinctions all the time. Think about an e-mail you had to read more than once to capture the meaning with the right tone, or a section of a book because you spaced out or were completely shocked by what the author said, so you read it again. Failing to reread text is a widespread problem that happens in classrooms everywhere. Reading closely can help with this issue.

The other part of the problem is the lack of purposeful planning behind the use of texts and questions. When teachers take the time to truly think about their content standards, as well as how they will measure when students arrive at mastery of those standards, then instructional practices become more intentional and students participate in the activity or assignment with a meaningful focus. The end result should be that students learn.

Teachers are not deliverers of information, nor are they teaching texts. Students are people, and people can learn without teachers dumping information on them, so how can you shift to being an instructional coach versus a dispenser of information?

One way to accomplish this change in instructional practice is to align your instruction to the grade level Common Core State Standards (CCSS). The new standards are a more rigorous set of expectations that will require teachers to change the way they instruct students to learn their content. If you do not teach language arts or reading, then you can think of the English/Language Arts (ELA) standards as performance standards or life skills. Students will need to be able to understand how to utilize their thinking for any form of literacy (media, social media, advertisement, historical events, scientific information, e-mail, etc.).

For example, College and Career Readiness Anchor Standard 8 for Reading states high school graduates need to be able to look at a source of information and determine the validity and sufficiency of the represented evidence. This is a life skill. People are inundated with advertisements, infomercials, e-mails, and business deals. If they do not learn how to evaluate these forms of literacy, then it might cost them a lot of money, time, or possibly their livelihood.

A second way to help with the shift is to follow the backward planning process described in the previous chapter; you want to start by identifying your content standards and which embedded ELA standards will assist with processing, learning, and applying the content knowledge. Then decide how you will measure whether students have mastered the standards. Finally, what will you plan for the students to do (activities and/or assignments) to get there?

Lastly, reading closely will help with the shift. This chapter will provide you with another approach to help students interact with text multiple times. This approach to reading closely is called *Preview/Review*, but you can call it whatever you want. Accordingly this chapter will pick up building on the previous sixth grade science lesson—"compare and contrast types of infectious agents that may infect the human body, including viruses, bacteria, fungi, and parasites," (CPALMS, 2012, SC.6.L.14.6).

However, the complexity of the text and task will increase from the *Change Perspective* (chapter 2) lesson. You will see that each approach forces the students to dig deeper as well as challenges the students with more complex text at or above their grade level.

As a reminder, though, when you choose to use a text to move students toward mastery of standards, the teacher must go through the "cold" read and "expert" read during the planning process. The teacher should time him/herself reading at each step and double or triple the time for students based on how quickly s/he is able to read. The teacher should never give students text that s/he has not read and reread first because the teacher cannot be surprised by the text; this is a nonnegotiable.

PLANNING FOR PREVIEW/REVIEW

Preview/review is the second approach for reading closely, which helps students understand there are patterns of organization to informational text that will aid them in understanding the explicit meaning of text in order to later analyze for deeper meaning. This reading closely approach lends itself nicely during testing situations too and when interacting with longer text. Focusing on the text structure enables readers to easily maneuver through text, answer questions, and truly follow the author's point.

This particular approach has students interact with the text three to five times in order to process connections, relationships, and patterns depending on how deep you want students to go with the text. The first interaction with the text is to set a learning objective, provide brief background knowledge and/or front-load vocabulary, and have students preview the text.

In the second interaction with the text, the teacher asks the students to do a cold read of the entire text. During the third interaction with the text, the teacher sets a purpose for the students to do an expert read, still connected to the learning objective but requiring students to build a table of contents in the margins of the text in order to identify evidence connected to overall structure. Students will then share identified evidence and implications with a partner and finally with the entire class in order to process their understanding.

For the fourth interaction with the text, the teacher models text-dependent questions and then has students work with a partner to practice text-dependent questions. Always bring the class back together to gauge their level of practice and validate thinking. If you choose to venture into a fifth interaction with the text (addressed further in chapter 5), then you will have students analyze the text for integration of knowledge and ideas (text structures, word analysis, relationships, etc.) and craft and structure (purpose, tone, structure, perspective, etc.), and this requires the students to venture back into the text for another expert read (refer back to chapter 1, figure 1.1, for the entire overview of reading closely).

For this instructional approach, preview/review, refer back to the sixth grade science standard mentioned previously—students will be able to "compare and contrast types of infectious agents that may infect the human body, including viruses, bacteria, fungi, and parasites" (CPALMS, 2012, SC.6.L.14.6).

Remember as an example, this is a four-week unit, and it started with the text described in chapter 2—"Bacteria: The Good, the Bad, and the Stinky" by Joy Masoff in *Read-Aloud Anthology* by Janet Allen and Patrick Daley (2004) in day 1. The second day of this unit of instruction, students watched a short video on bacteria and read a section in their textbook, which allowed them to validate and invalidate information in the text they read the day before and collect more evidence for the final summative assessment (a compare and contrast essay of infectious agents).

Now, the class is in the third day of instruction, and the learning moves into the use of an excerpt from *The Demon in the Freezer* by Richard Preston (2002), which will be followed by *The Black Death, 1348* (2001) from www.eyewitnesstohistory.com. As mentioned previously, you can always choose additional texts in order to set the stage for students to cross analyze and build knowledge from a diverse group of sources on all four parts of the standard (bacteria, viruses, fungi, and parasites).

As explained before, these texts are great activators to get the students interested in learning about science. Keep in mind, when you learn about new instructional practices, you want to adapt not adopt. One way to adapt this strategy could be to use it with your textbook. Another way to adapt is to only have the students do a preview as the cold read and then interact with the text during the first full read. The purpose is for students to learn how to identify text structures in order to analyze, interpret, evaluate, and synthesize information.

So, now you are ready to plan for reading closely to learn content-specific information. You will find a template to guide you through planning for preview/review, the second reading closely approach, in appendix C. Do not forget, once you choose the text, you must read the text. Again, too often teachers read assigned text for the first time with the students. This cannot happen because it does not allow teachers to plan for intentional teaching for intentional learning. If you want your students to do it, then you do it first. This will also allow you to confirm or negate your text choice based on your key standards.

Just like with change perspective, you want to number each paragraph and you want your students to do the same. This will allow for easy reference when students are discussing, supporting, or proving points. Then set a timer while you read the text, *The Demon in the Freezer* by Richard Preston (2002), through the first time. Again, if you are a fast reader, then you need to plan for students to require three times your clock. If you are a slower reader, then you need to plan for students to require two times your clock. For example, if you read this text in three minutes and thirty seconds, then consider your students and give them four to seven minutes for an initial read.

To reiterate, the cold read should be for familiarity for you during lesson planning and for the students during the interaction. You want to ensure a literal understanding of the text (What is the topic and what does the author want you to know about the topic?); students will be able to "read closely to determine what the text says explicitly" (College and Career Readiness Anchor Standards for Reading, p. 35).

Similar to the first approach, during your cold read, circle words you anticipate students might have difficulty with during their interaction with the text. This will allow you to front-load key vocabulary prior to reading in order to increase comprehension and minimize frustration for students who are not reading grade level text yet, or you can plan a mini activity for students to work with the key words, such as *sounds like* and *looks like*, prior to reading. For more ideas about vocabulary, you can read *Teaching Vocabulary in All Classrooms* (3rd ed.) by Camille Blachowicz and Peter J. Fisher (2006). Remember, spending time with previewing vocabulary should take less than five minutes of your class time.

Now, think about what is important for students to know about this text, understand about this text, and do with the information from this text based on your content-specific grade level standards. What is the desired effect or outcome? How will using this text help students understand and master the standards? This will drive your learning objective. It will also drive your decision to briefly front-load background information and key vocabulary.

However, keep in mind the purpose of facilitating learning for students is to move them toward independence, because during tests and real life, no one will be there to build background knowledge or front-load vocabulary. Therefore, this should be gradually released back to the student to take ownership of as the year progresses and students work toward mastery of grade level standards.

The next step in your planning process is to read the texts for an expert read. This time as you read, think about the text structure(s) the author uses to make a point or describe/explain information, as well as the main message detailed throughout. There are several different text structures, such as compare and contrast, cause and effect, problem and solution, generalization and example, definition and example, process, time order, and enumeration or listing.

The type of text structure will lead what is extracted from the text and noted in the margin during the expert read or the review read. This becomes notes in the margins or a table of contents that students will be able to use to answer questions, have discussions, or use in their summative assessment. The reason for this marginal approach to reading is to stimulate interaction with text and discussion among students that will require them to cite evidence from the text to prove their perspective, which gets them ready for argumentative writing and debates, so students will be able "to make logical inferences from it; cite specific textual evidence when writing or speaking to support conclusions drawn from the text" (College and Career Readiness Anchor Standards for Reading, p. 35).

Another type of marginal annotation is simply summarizing the text. This is actually the easiest to start students out with because summarizing is a skill they have used since kindergarten. Students simply read each paragraph and quickly jot down three to five words in the margin of the main point and key detail presented in each paragraph. Once they are used to this type of text interaction, then move to pulling out the text structure with interpretation and synthesis in the margins. Table 3.1 offers several text structures (patterns of organization) students can identify and use to interact with when making

Table 3.1. Options of Text Structures

Patterns of Organization for Text Structures

- Enumeration or Listing
- Time Order or Sequence of Events
- Cause and Effect
- Compare and Contrast
- Problem and Solution
- Definition and Example
- Classification or Categorization
- Process

marginal notes to summarize the author's message or prepare to argue a point using the author's details within the text structure.

The marginal notes you ask students to generate for the expert read should be connected to your grade level standards, move students toward an understanding of the learning objective, and provide students a reason to move from a literal understanding of text to a critical understanding of text. You do not want students to make surface notes in the margin, such as a heart, a smiley face, or an exclamation mark. This is not in-depth thinking nor does it lead to deep thinking.

You do not always have to use a pattern of organization for the expert read. You may ask students to summarize or pull out details that get at a driving question, which will lead to discussion. The most important thing to remember is to have students look at the text with a different purpose from their first interaction with the text. If you have students read text multiple times for different reasons, then they will be better equipped to pay more attention to the details around them and be better prepared for interaction in the real world rather than feel isolated and stuck to their current situation. In addition, it keeps students focused and active when they have to read long and/or boring text.

The end in mind with preview/review, a reading closely approach, is to have students drive the entire interaction by the fourth quarter. They conduct the cold read. They choose the purpose of the expert read connected to the learning objective, and they facilitate the discussion amongst peers. This helps students move toward the final reading standard, "read and comprehend complex literary and informational texts independently and proficiently" (College and Career Readiness Anchor Standards for Reading, p. 35).

Just like in the previous chapter, students may read to "assess how point of view or purpose shapes the content and style of a text" (College and Career Readiness Anchor Standards for Reading, p. 35), or how individuals, events, or ideas impact the central message. Students can identify the author's word choice (negative, positive, or neutral) and how those choices impact the text structure, as well as the point the author is attempting to make, which leads students to analyze how this works together to shape the meaning or message of the text, citing to be right.

In the text mentioned earlier, *The Demon in the Freezer* by Richard Preston (2002), have students identify the mixed patterns used as well as the descriptive language chosen to depict the event in order to help the reader understand how this virus affected human beings. Of course, this is directly connected back to the standard also mentioned earlier; students will be able to "compare and contrast types of infectious agents that may infect the human body, including viruses, bacteria, fungi, and parasites" (CPALMS, 2012, SC.6.L.14.6).

Now you are ready to develop questions that challenge students at different levels of cognitive complexity. Look back at chapter 2 to review the different levels, and remember as the year progresses and the rigor of the task and complexity of the text increases, so should the expectation of the cognitive demand. Your students will rise to whatever bar you set for them, so set it high and put scaffolds in place to help those who need a little more support along the way.

Remember, it is also worth mentioning again to set students up to be text dependent when they answer all types of questions. You can model this type of response to questions as needed once students have practiced a few times, but at this point, differentiation is the best approach. Most students should be working toward independence, but for those who need more explicit instruction and guided practice, continue to model how to think through different types of questions, go back into the text to cite to be right, and triangulate information.

Even opportunities to process information must be purposefully planned. Once students have worked through questions, citing evidence to support their responses, remember to give them time to process those choices with a partner or in small groups. You can follow this with a whole-class share out in order to gauge their understanding and discussion.

Finally, think about how you will check for understanding at the end of the class. This is important because it will drive what you choose to have the class work through the next day. A check for understanding can be done in many different ways; for example, students can mark where they are on a scale aligned to the learning objective and explain with evidence why. Another quick way to check for understanding is to use technology, such as students using their cell phones to send their responses while Socrative (http://www.socrative.com/) collects and charts the live incoming data.

In the next section of this chapter, you will read about how this lesson unfolds in a sixth grade classroom. Appendix D also offers additional lesson plans for intermediate and high school, so you can refer to those samples as well when you are planning for this instructional practice.

TEACHING PREVIEW/REVIEW

For this scenario, the same sixth grade teacher uses reading closely, preview/review approach, with the excerpt *The Demon in the Freezer* by Richard Preston (2002). Notice how she uses this text to build on the same content standard but still gradually releases the responsibility to the students throughout the lesson. The lesson can take anywhere from fifty to seventy minutes, depending on your students, how comfortable you are with the process, how long the text is, and how much "teacher talk" occurs. Now step into Ms. Williams's classroom.

The rain is coming down in sheets all around, so the students are flying through the door quickly. This is a nice change from barely making it just as the bell sounds. Conversations occur all through the class as students whisper about their weekends and the teacher continues to stand at the door and greet those still running in from the rain. Finally the late bell rings and all the students routinely take their seats and become focused on the learning objective, "Students will be able to identify how viruses spread and impact living organisms."

"The past couple of days we discussed the differences between bacteria that are helpful and harmful to the human body. Now, we'll discuss the way viruses help or harm human beings. Remember at the end of this unit, you'll synthesize your understanding of how types of infectious agents do or do not infect the human body using evidence from the multiple sources you interact with over the four weeks," Ms. Williams begins.

"Today, we'll start our discovery with an excerpt from *The Demon in the Freezer* by Richard Preston. You'll also learn a new way to interact with text today that will help you monitor your comprehension and deepen your understanding for discussion as well as for your synthesis at the end," the teacher takes the time to explain.

"Let's start like we always do and number our paragraphs," Ms. Williams directs. "Show me with your fingers how many paragraphs you identified." Students all around the room display four fingers.

"Great, there are four. Now, there are a few words I want to bring to your attention before you start to read. I have them here on this chart paper so you can refer to them anytime you come to them in the text. I'll read them and you'll circle or highlight them in your text. *Entangled* is in paragraph 1, sentence 1, and it means 'intertwine,'" she quickly points out.

"*Affinity* is in paragraph 1, sentence 4, and it means 'liking.' *Infectious* you will also find in paragraph 1, sentence 5, and it means 'contagious.' *Eradicated* follows in the same paragraph, next sentence, and it means 'erase,'" Ms. Williams briefly explains along with five additional key words.

"Now this reading closely approach starts us off with a preview of the text. In the preview, we want to pay attention to text features, such as the title, captions, pictures, and bold words." Ms. Williams demonstrates the preview process out loud. She reads the title and author. Then she reads the entire first paragraph, the first sentence of paragraphs 2 and 3, and finishes by reading the entire last paragraph.

"Now, turn to your shoulder partner and the person who is taller will tell their partner what the topic is, and the shorter partner will tell what the author wants the reader to know about that topic. Go!"

Students are given one minute to complete this task. "The topic is the smallpox virus," Katherine says while facing her shoulder partner.

"The author is going to tell us about two strands of this virus," Josh says back to his shoulder partner, who is nodding her head in agreement.

Then the teacher brings them back together and asks for volunteers to share out their thinking. There are many ways you can do this. You can ask for each student to write his/her response on a mini whiteboard and hold it up. You can have students text their answers using Poll Everywhere or Socrative, which are free resource tools online, as well as application tools you can get on iPads, iPods, or smartphones. The way to share information to check for understanding and inform instruction is truly limited only by your ability to imagine and try new approaches.

Once you ensure all students have an explicit meaning of the text (CCSS RI.6.1), then they are ready to move into a cold read. During the cold read this time, you will provide them with a clear purpose for reading, since they have already become familiar with the text during the preview. "Now we will engage in a cold read and focus on the details to support the main idea. Let's count off 1, 2, and 3 for the purpose." Ms. Williams leads the students in counting off.

"One."

"Two."

"Three," the students call out all around the room until each student is assigned a number.

"Good. Ones, you will read for the what, which are the details pertaining to the different strands or the main idea. Twos, you will read for the symptoms of the what, and threes, you will read for the results of the what. Be prepared to support your thinking. Okay, someone tell me what I've just asked you to do during the cold read," Ms. Williams asks.

She calls on a student from the front: "Well, like I'm gonna read to find out what the author means by smallpox virus."

"I'm going to read to find out how someone would know if they have this virus, like signs," one from the middle says.

"Yeah, so I'll read to find out how it ends for people who get the virus," another student from the back of the room says to quickly reiterate the directions and purpose of the cold read. Then the students are given seven minutes to complete the task.

Once the time is up, the teacher has the students get into groups of three made up of a one, a two, and a three in order to discuss findings and implications of those findings (CCSS RI.6.1). Students take time to discuss implications derived from explicit and inferred meaning based on their focus. This will help them analyze relationships between and among sentences and paragraphs later (CCSS RI.6.5).

"Who wants to go first?" Jessica asks.

"Let's just go in order," Josh says.

"Fine, so the smallpox virus is like a parasite that has two types. There's the black pox, which is super deadly, and there's the smallpox, but that one can lead to death too," Katherine explains her what.

"According to the text, some signs of the smallpox virus are fever, broken skin, pus, and bleeding, which is really gross," Jessica tells her group.

"I thought it was cool!" Josh expresses.

"You would," Jessica retorts.

"Okay. So in some cases the author says people can survive, but doctors claim if the skin raises all over the body, then the person will die for sure, and black pox always ends with death," Josh explains.

"The conversations I hear are on task and moving toward hypotheses, which I know we will continue to explore this week in multiple sources along with our textbooks. Let's move into our expert read. As you participate in the expert read, you'll create a table of contents in the margins that briefly summarizes key details in three to five words or less and will serve as evidence to refer back to as you move forward with supporting your hypotheses about causes and effects of pathogens. Let me show you what this looks like," Ms. Williams offers to model.

Ms. Williams reads the entire first paragraph, which explains how the virus got started and the implications of that cause. She then writes the detail or evidence that supports the presented information in the margins of the text, *virus jumped from an animal*. She follows this with challenging the students to turn to their partner to try the process before they do it independently.

"Partners sitting on the right read the paragraph out loud and partners on the left think out loud after the reading of what you'll write and why." This extra step ensures students truly understand how to interact with the text during the expert read. Students are challenged to read the last two paragraphs on their own.

The table of contents is connected to standards and is a way to compare and contrast across multiple sources on a topic or theme without the need to reread the entire text three to five days later when students are pulling together a synthesis of learning with evidence from different texts. Although the marginal notes serve as a quick summary of each paragraph, which will allow readers to quickly skim for answers to guarantee accuracy of text evidence for question, the marginal notes can also be connected to an ELA purpose. For example, the table of contents is maybe used to identify facts and opinions in order to prepare for a Socrative circle or written response. The purpose for the marginal notes should be driven by the learning goal.

After a sufficient amount of time, bring students back together to share their thinking and the why behind their thinking. They can do this with a partner, small group, or whole class. The most important piece of information to walk away with is how important the process time is for students, so do not skip it. Remember to model every piece the first time students experience something and then gradually transfer the responsibility of the cognitive load.

Reading closely is about diving into a text multiple times to deepen one's understanding and process through collaborative discussion (listening and speaking) in order to independently answer text-dependent questions. So the last interaction with this text is to challenge students to think critically; analyze the word choice, sentence structures, and text structure; and cite evidence when answering questions that require students to draw conclusions and make inferences. When you first ask students to interact with text-dependent questions, remember to model and think aloud and then release the cognitive responsibility gradually in order to build self-efficacy and independence.

Finally, think about how you will check for understanding to inform instruction as you move forward with the standards. You can use a ticket out the door that requires students to respond with a short answer using text evidence. Appendix E has a sample ticket out the door you can use with your students, but think about moving toward digital responses, such as Collaborize Classroom (http://www.collaborizeclassroom.com/) or Edmodo (https://www.edmodo.com/), which are both free platforms. Table 3.2 provides you with a scale to measure CCSS Reading Informational Text, Key Ideas and Details, standard 1. You are looking for students to state an opinion, state the source, and provide one to three pieces of textual evidence to support their answer.

FINAL THOUGHT

When students have a difficult time reading text, there are several reasons for the "why," but this approach allows for students to take control of the

Table 3.2. Sample Writing Response Rubric

CCR Anchor Standards

Writing

1. Write arguments to support claims in an analysis of substantive topics or texts, using valid reasoning and relevant and sufficient evidence.

Reading

1. Read closely to determine what the text says explicitly and to make logical inferences from it; cite specific textual evidence when writing or speaking to support conclusions drawn from the text.
2. Determine central ideas or themes of a text and analyze their development; summarize the key supporting details and ideas.
10. Read and comprehend complex literary and informational texts independently and proficiently.

Score	1	2	3	4
Description of scoring	Misconception—Written response demonstrates a statement/opinion unrelated to the text.	Written response is on topic and contains a statement/opinion related to the text.	Written response is on topic, includes a statement/opinion with at least one detail/fact from the text that directly supports statement **OR** the source is provided to support statement.	Written response is on topic, includes a statement/opinion directly supported with details/facts from the text, and location/source of evidence is cited.

Source: College and Career Readiness Anchor Standards for Reading, p. 35.

reading process, making it more manageable. This reading closely approach truly helps students when text is boring, too long, or layered with complexity.

Students explore the text four times in order to gain an understanding. This is not a process that can be taught two weeks before a test; it must be modeled, practiced, and used over a long stretch of time in order to become proficient and see the benefits. This leads to the most important pieces needed for any learning process, tracking progress. Have students read and answer questions at the start of the year their own way. Then teach them each of the different reading closely approaches each quarter.

At the end of each quarter, challenge the student to read and answer questions to a different grade level passage using the current reading closely approach. Finally, have them chart their results each time. They will see improvement; that's the best part!

Chapter Four

Game Changer with Strategic Approach

When you think about the importance of the need to ensure all students leave public education fully capable of collaboration, creative thinking, critical thinking, and communication, the demand becomes clear to increase the rigor and set higher expectations while also nurturing individualized interests and talents. These are the new literacy skills of tomorrow; they will help students successfully thrive in a world that is not yet known.

Unfortunately, the reality is that some students will always need extra support in order to reach the end in mind. Do not fret, though. Think about every year when April rolls around, and no matter how many times someone walks you through doing your taxes, you seem to always need extra support to make it happen. The important point to remember here is not to get frustrated or discouraged as you continue to support some students more than others. Focus on whether students are making gains at an accelerated rate in order to close the gap and are prepared to embark on a life in a world that is globally connected.

Using the reading closely approaches described in chapters 2 and 3 as well as the third approach introduced and explained in this chapter will aid you in fully supporting each and every student who struggles with reading to be able to truly go deeper into text through multiple reads, collaborative processing, communication and clarification of meaning, and interaction with text multiple times and in multiple ways in order to think critically and creatively about a wide range of literacies.

Literacy is no longer about teaching students how to read; it is about teaching students how to interact with the presentation of ideas, opinions, arguments, suggestions, and ongoing access to information in the world all around them beyond the black-and-white print on a sheet of paper.

However, no matter how great these instructional approaches are, if they are not used by a teacher who intentionally plans for learning, uses appropriate practices at the right time and with the right students, as well as problem-solves around students' response to instruction, then all of this information is a moot point.

So without further ado, chapter 4 brings to you—the game changer of reading closely—*Strategic Approach*. This approach is the most difficult to intentionally plan for as well as for students to utilize; however, the desired effect is truly worth every drop of sweat.

The best time to use this approach is with a longer, more complex text in which students will engage in difficult concepts or skills. You can plan to use this reading closely approach to start a unit or in the middle of the unit, based on your students' needs. The approach challenges students to dive into a text four to six times, building upon their understanding and narrowing their focus to support a final conclusion, argument, position, or thesis. It generally takes about two to three class periods of instruction, but the outcome should be huge!

To prepare for the planning process, select your lead standards. These are the main standards that will drive your students' learning process. They are also the standards that you will provide direct and explicit instruction on, as well as plan for meaningful practice around.

Then determine which standards will need to be included to support the lead standards. These standards may need to be addressed at varying levels based on your students' needs. Next, determine how you will assess students' mastery of the lead and/or supporting standards. Will you create a paper and pencil test? Will you have them write a final paper? Will you ask them to put something together or design something?

Ultimately, you are led to choose texts. This is an area where many teachers struggle. Hours of valuable time can be sacrificed to find the perfect text. However, there are several online websites that offer help in this area. Some websites where you can access text are,

- Teen Ink—articles written by teens for teens (http://www.teenink.com/nonfiction/)
- ReadWorks—nonfiction texts, lessons, and ideas (http://www.readworks.org/)

- Tween Tribune—relevant articles written for kids of all ages (http://tweentribune.com/)
- News ELA—current news articles on important topics (https://newsela.com)
- Author and educator Kelly Gallagher—provides an article of the week (http://kellygallagher.org/resources/articles.html)

So this chapter will continue to build on the previous sixth grade science lessons—"compare and contrast types of infectious agents that may infect the human body, including viruses, bacteria, fungi, and parasites" (CPALMS, 2012, SC.6.L.14.6). However, the complexity of the text and task will increase from the preview/review (chapter 3) lesson. You will see that each approach challenges the students to dig deeper as well as confronts the students with more complex text at their grade level.

As a reminder, though, when you choose to use a text to move students toward mastery of standards, the teacher must go through the "cold" read and the "expert" read during the planning process. The teacher should time him/herself reading at each step and double or triple the time for students based on how quickly s/he is able to read. The teacher should never give students text that s/he has not read and reread first, because the teacher cannot be surprised by the text; this is a nonnegotiable. To act against this is malpractice, and that is not okay.

PLANNING FOR STRATEGIC APPROACH

Anytime you begin the planning process, you start with the focus standards. These are the main standards you will provide direct and explicit instruction for throughout the unit of instruction. Then you will need to unpack the lead standards in order to determine which supporting standards may need to be addressed so that students are able to master the lead standards at an analysis level or higher. You may wish to break the standards into what students need to know, do, and understand in order to demonstrate mastery of the standards.

Ultimately, this will drive you to identify necessary vocabulary and knowledge along the lines of taxonomy students will need to do as well.

For this example, the lead standard is "compare and contrast types of infectious agents that may infect the human body, including viruses, bacteria, fungi, and parasites" (CPALMS, 2012, SC.6.L.14.6), and the supporting standards are CCSS ELA RI.6.1, RI.6.6, W.6.1a-e, and SL.6.1a-d (http://www.corestandards.org/). It is important to note, though, if your students lack the ability to utilize the skills within the supporting standards, then direct instruction with meaningful practice must take place around the supporting standards too.

From this point in the planning process, you will be able to create a scale on the main standards for students to be able to track their learning progression as well as for you to informatively assess where students are in mastering the grade level expectations. Then create your learning target that students will be able to do by the end of the lesson within the overall unit of instruction. For more information on planning units of instructions with learning goals and scales, you can read *Using Common Core Standards to Enhance Classroom Instruction & Assessment* by Robert Marzano, David C. Yanuski, Jan K. Hoegh, and Julie Simms (2013).

For the purpose of this planning example, the learning target is, "I am able to identify and explain different types of infectious agents and analyze how different agents impact human beings." The learning objective is in student-friendly language and represents the 3.0 on the scale. The 2.0 on the scale defines what the student is able to identify and explain about certain viruses, bacteria, fungi, and parasites. A student is a 1.0 on the scale if s/he struggles with the 2.0 and needs prompting and support to be partially successful. Students are considered to be at the 4.0 if they are able to independently apply skills during self-selection and apply them during research, experimentation, or inquiry, and transfer to life application as well as teach peers.

Now, choose the curriculum resources you will use to move students toward mastery. In the scenario described in the next section, the learning will take place around a text from www.eyewitnesstohistory.com, *The Black Death, 1348* (2001). This text is chosen to hook students, activate thinking, and drive discussion that will lead to inquiry learning later in the unit. The way students will interact with this text is through reading closely using strategic approach. The planning template for this reading closely approach is located in appendix F and will guide you through the process described within this section of the chapter.

Start by reading the text while you time yourself. This way you know how much time needs to be allotted for a cold read. Keep in mind how quickly you read so you know whether you need to double or triple your time. The text used for this example was read in eleven minutes by a moderate-pace reader, so the time should be rounded or doubled for students. Now, read it again to determine the text structure, interesting points, and details. You need to make sure the text will help move students toward comparing and contrasting infectious agents or whatever your learning target identifies.

In order to accomplish this expectation, texts should provide characteristics or signs and results or effects of each presented infectious agent so that students can use text evidence to support their analysis. Students have already read the previous two texts described early in this text as well as read sections within their textbooks. They are collecting evidence along the way in order to draw a final conclusion about infectious agents.

This particular text lends itself to cause and effect; however, the causes are implicit, which makes the text structure much more complex. Therefore, a mini-lesson on explicit and implicit (inferences) may need to be taught in order for students to be able to read closely. You may also need to quickly go over a few words, such as *rampage, unprecedented, pestilence, interrelated, manifestation, pneumatic, septicemia,* and *ignorantly* for students to be successful reading grade level text independently during a cold read. Once those pieces are prepared and planned, you are ready to mark the text. You want to mark evidences or details that support causes with a C and evidences or details that support effects with an E throughout the entire text.

After the text is marked for cause and effect, think about how those details identified can be categorized into broader topics, because the point is for them to compare and contrast across multiple literacies at the end of the unit, so it will be easier if they begin to categorize their evidence. For example, for this text, the categories (ignorance, living conditions, and encounters) can be about how infectious agents make their way into the human body, which will help with the end in mind of the unit. Students can also go back to past texts to categorize their findings into one of the three categories. You can even have students think about characteristics, results, and treatments as categories over the multiple literacies.

Finally, think about a question that can start broad and opinion based but can be changed for students to draw a final conclusion and support it with text-based evidence. For example, for this text, you can start by asking, "Based on what you know right now, what needs to happen for an infectious agent to take control of a human body, and what happens once an infectious agent takes control?" This type of question allows for opinions to be shared, which promotes thinking and discussion. There is no right or wrong answer at this point, because students have not read the text yet.

However, by the end of the lesson, students will be able to come to a final conclusion, and the question will be worded differently for less interpretation and opinion and more geared toward an answer with evidence. For example, the question at the end of the class may be restated as, "According to the text, which factor most likely causes the spread of viruses and the contamination or death of a human body?"

This planning process takes at least an hour and requires a lot of thinking on your part, but the outcome from students is well worth every single second of planning. You will not want to use this approach with every text. Remember anything can be bad if it is overused, so think about using this approach once a quarter and with longer, more difficult text where students would need additional scaffolds to be successful in the end.

TEACHING STRATEGIC APPROACH

Think about the following scenario as a sixth grade teacher uses reading closely, strategic approach, with a text from online, *The Black Death, 1348*, from EyeWitness to History (2001). Read about how the teacher uses this text to build on the same content standard but still gradually releases the responsibility to the students throughout the lesson. The lesson can take anywhere from fifty to one hundred minutes, depending on your students, how comfortable you are with the process, how long the text is, and how much "teacher talk" occurs.

The following scenario takes place in a middle school with 22 percent diversity and 29 percent low socioeconomic status. Although the students who attend this school generally come from affluent families, only 71 percent of students demonstrated proficiency on the state reading assessment. There is a need for an increase of time spent reading and interacting with text at all schools, not just the schools with high numbers of economically disadvantaged. If schools were really hitting the mark, then this school full of affluent families would score above 90 percent.

Ms. Williams is at her desk checking some last-minute e-mails as the minute hand strikes the seven and the first bell rings to start the day. She slowly stands and stretches as she takes in one last deep breath and releases it just as the first set of students swing open the classroom door and flood in ready to start the day ahead. "Good morning," she says to the three students as she steps over to the door and holds it open to welcome the rest of her class.

"Zaria, love the new haircut!" Ms. Williams exclaims.

"Thanks."

"Steven, did you remember to bring that book back you borrowed, because Sergio is waiting for it?" Ms. Williams inquires.

"Yeah, I've got it here in my book bag."

The sound of the loud bell vibrates through the halls and into the classes to signal it is time to really get down to business. "Okay, okay, let's get started. Your warm-up is on the whiteboard." The warm-up asks them a question to activate their thinking and is directly connected to the learning target.

Warm-up: In your opinion, how easily can you pick up an infectious agent?

The teacher gives students two minutes to respond to this in writing. Then she asks them to turn to their shoulder partners and discuss their opinions. Finally she takes a poll to find out the class's opinions. The entire process takes about five minutes.

"Davonte, what did you and your partner think?" the teacher wonders.

"Well, we were thinking you probably pick up bacteria everywhere, but like viruses come from other people who are sick," Davonte shares.

"How did that person get the virus to share, and is it always a virus that makes you sick?" Ms. Williams questions.

"I don't know. We sort of talked about that; maybe eating something with it on it."

"What does everyone else think?"

"We said some of the same things, but we were thinking like you know from animals like in that piece we read about smallpox," Sergio adds.

"I like the way you are referencing other texts we've read this unit," Ms. Williams encourages.

After about five minutes, Ms. Williams brings the class back together to dig deeper now and move from just their opinions to text-based evidence for support. "Before we dig deeper to find evidence to support our thinking, let's look at a few words you may come to and not know. I don't want these words to hinder your ability to build knowledge and think critically. Number your paragraphs," she directs the class.

"Show me with your fingers how many paragraphs you counted."

Two arms shoot up around the room showing one finger on the left hand and five fingers on the right. "Excellent, there are fifteen paragraphs. No one was tricked by the subheadings.

"There are a few words I want to bring to your attention. They're important words that you need to know in order to understand the text, but today is about reading, so I'm going to simply reveal those words and their meanings so you can read without too much difficulty. I'll point them out to you in the text, and you circle them with your writing utensil," Ms. Williams explains. She quickly highlights ten key words and has them defined on a chart paper for students to refer back to at any time during their reading. Ms. Williams has the students circle the words in the text so when they are reading, they know that word is defined for them on the chart paper. This takes about five minutes.

Ms. Williams explains to the students that they will engage in a cold read. While they read, they will mark up the text using the activator question as a framework for their learning. Advanced students will look for all pieces of evidence to support the question, but students who struggle with reading should only look for one and share with a partner. This can be shifted as you move students toward mastery of grade level standards throughout the school year.

"During the cold read, I want you to consider the question you responded to during the warm-up. As you interact with this text for the first time, you'll mark for evidence to support your opinion or challenge your opinion. The text structure will help guide us with finding evidence," the teacher begins to explain.

"So shoulder partners on the right, your right, when you're reading, you will mark evidence that supports the causes of infectious agents entering the human body. The partner to the left will mark for evidence that supports the effects of infectious agents entering the human body. These pieces of evidence will be added to what we've already gathered from the three other texts and our textbooks when we do our final compare and contrast analysis. Let me show you what this looks like," Ms. Williams offers.

"Put your finger next to paragraph 1. Follow along as I read aloud," she directs the students. Then she reads paragraph 1. "The second sentence is marked with a C because it is the event that takes place, and the last sentence is marked with an E because it is the result of the event. Now, complete paragraph 2 on your own and we'll come back to discuss it before we mark up the entire text."

She gives them two minutes to read paragraph 2 and mark the text. Then she asks them to share their thinking with their shoulder partner as she walks around. "Okay, let's bring it together. Tell me what you and your partner discussed about paragraph 2," Ms. Williams probes.

"So we don't think there's any cause and effect in this paragraph," Zaria shares.

"Tell me more about why you think this," the teachers questions.

"Well, cause it's just listing the different forms. Like in the first sentence," John jumps in to explain.

"Does anyone else think this?"

Heads bob up and down all across the classroom.

"Well, I think that paragraph needs another look with a new lens," Ms. Williams says with a smile. "Let's look at it again and think about actions and results. Then I'll have you try one more paragraph before you work on this independently."

Ms. Williams walks around as students reread paragraph 2.

"Tell me your thoughts."

"It does have tons of results, like explaining what happens after someone gets the virus," Zaria says.

"But it don't have actions, you know who got it or how they got it," Devon adds.

"You're right. In this paragraph the cause or action is implied but the effect or result is clearly stated," Ms. Williams explains. "We need to remember what we learned about inferences while we read the rest of this article, because that will help us. Great job going back with an expert's eye and making that discovery. Okay, read the third paragraph and then we'll talk about it."

She gives the students one minute to read paragraph 3, which is made up of only one compound sentence. "So?"

"They don't know what causes the infection," Sergio says.

"Yeah, but once they get it, they are 'devastated,' so that's the result . . . I mean the effect," Steven offers.

"Are a result and an effect the same thing?"

"I think so because they both mean the end, right . . . ?" Steven half says and half questions.

"I'm asking you all, Steven," Ms. Williams challenges back.

"Then yes, I think they mean the same," Sergio answers.

"How do you know?"

"So a result means what you get at the end, and an effect is the result of something that happens," William adds to the conversation.

"I believe you're ready to do your cold read with this text. Remember to mark for either causes or effects and be prepared to share your findings with your partner. I'll give you eleven minutes."

While the students read, the teacher circulates the room to express the importance of this reading and be available if a student needs assistance. After the designated time, the teacher asks the students to share with their shoulder partner their findings. "Trade color pens with your partner. Now, readers who identified causes share with your partner and have your partner mark those places in the text, and then tell you what the effect of that cause is based on the text. When you're done, both of you should have your text marked for causes and effects, but be prepared to justify your thinking."

As the students share, the teacher walks around to verify students get it and if they do not, she can bring them back together after the four minutes to clarify any misconceptions. Some students do struggle with explicit meaning, so with a little class discussion they can bring it together enough to dive back into the text for an expert read. Students need to know that good readers interact with text multiple times to truly get something out of it.

Another adaptation is to have students just do the cold read without marking the text in order to become familiar first. Then ask them to do a second read as an expert to mark the text for the text structure. You can give them the text structure at first, but as the year progresses, think about shifting the cognitive load to the students and challenging them to identify the text structure and cite evidence.

During the expert read, students will take the evidence for the text structure and organize it into category topics. Again, you will start by providing them with the categories to organize their evidence, but as the year progresses, they should create those categories and support their thinking with evidence. Remember the categories are driven by the standards expressed as a learning target, activator, or essential question—*According to the text, what is the number one cause for the spread of infectious agents amongst human beings*? It is always the same question, but it is presented in several different ways, forcing the students to make a final decision or commitment and support it with evidence.

"So now you're going to go back through the text with a refined expert lens and specifically analyze your text markings to determine which category your evidence falls into. The first category is ignorance. If you classify your evidence under this category, you are saying the people caught the infectious agent because they didn't know anything about it. The second category is living conditions. If you believe your evidence goes under this category, then you believe their environment caused the spread. The final category is encounters. If your text markings belong under this category, then you are saying the virus spread due to encounters with other humans, so you will place your evidence here.

"Let me show you what this looks like. Put your finger on paragraph 3. Follow along. 'Having no defense and no understanding of the cause. . . . ' So because the people didn't know, I would mark this cause as ignorance," Ms. Williams thinks aloud. "Your turn to jump back through the text and categorize your text structure evidence."

The students take eleven minutes to read back through the text with an expert lens, focusing in on their evidence already identified from the pattern of organization, and think about each piece in terms of categories. "Now, turn to your shoulder partner and share how you categorized your text structure evidence. Then listen as your partner shares with you. The partner whose first name is closest to A in the alphabet shares first," the teacher directs the students after reading a third time. As the students share with a partner, the teacher walks around and listens to their conversation. This lets her know if they got it, how much did they get, or do they need a little more direction.

"Okay, let's come back together. I heard some great categorizing conversation. How about we share some with the whole group? Zaria . . . ," Ms. Williams calls on to start.

"Well, pretty much all of paragraph 5, because it uses the word *ignorant* several times. No one knew much of anything, not even the doctors. That's scary," Zaria adds.

"But it wasn't just people who didn't know, because in paragraph 6, it says 'the sick communicated it to the healthy who came near them,' so it's not like they were avoiding them. I'm not hanging around no sick people anymore," Sergio interjects.

"Yeah, but in paragraph 8, the rich were able to avoid the sick easier, so that would mean their living conditions. I don't think that's fair," Davonte jumps into the conversation.

"What's not fair?" Ms. Williams questions.

"You know, the rich don't get sick just because they have all the luxury . . . paragraph 8 talks about how they 'shut themselves up in houses where there were no sick.' Why should they avoid sickness just because they have money?"

"Do you think money buys health now?" Ms. Williams asks.

"I don't know," James says.

"I guess," Stephanie murmurs.

"Why?" Ms. Williams inquires.

"If I get sick and don't have money to see a doctor, then how can I get better?" Stephanie explains.

"You don't always need to see a doctor. I had a cold last year and my mom just made me rest, but I didn't go to a doctor," James retorts.

"So it depends on how sick you are, right?" Stephanie wonders.

"These are excellent questions that I have captured for us so we can explore them further as we continue to spend time learning about infectious agents. I believe we are just about out of time. Here is your ticket out the door. According to the text, which category caused the virus to spread, contaminate, and kill the most human beings? How does this evidence prove or disprove your opinion from the start of class? I'll give you five minutes to answer this question. Great class today, and come prepared to dig deeper into our unit tomorrow. I'll stand by the door for you to hand your ticket out the door to me as you exit with the sounding of the bell," Ms. Williams explains.

Students spend the full five minutes jotting down their answers and referring back to the text to cite evidence to support their final conclusion. Ms. Williams will hold on to these for the end of the unit so students can have them for their final assessment.

FINAL THOUGHT

Oftentimes students do not want to read text that they see as irrelevant to them. By finding the relevance through curiosity built by high-interest texts, students begin to naturally dig deeper into the topic they are studying. Appendix G offers two additional sample lessons for strategic approach, one for a seventh grade civics class and the other for a fourth grade social studies class.

Students dig into a text multiple times to read closely in order to truly understanding the explicit and implicit meaning of the text. It is important for students to realize and understand that good readers read difficult or challenging text several times to learn from it and expand their understanding. This takes time and practice, which means students must read texts to learn and not just be spoon-fed information to pass a test or make it through the class.

Of course, remember to also challenge your students to answer questions using text evidence as each piece of text brings new challenges and gets slightly more difficult. Have them process thinking with peers and reflect on their thinking in order for true learning to happen. Utilizing the reading closely approaches describe in the previous two chapters and in this one will help them meet those challenges and find success in the end. Finally, have them continue to chart their results each time, because they will see improvement; that's the best part!

Chapter Five

Stretch into High Cognitive Literacy Tasks

Imagine you sit down in front of your computer in your quiet office and you click your Internet browser, summoning the world all around you to be available at the touch of your fingertips. To critically maneuver around this world and not be hacked, scammed, or led astray, you must be literate in the digital world, which requires you to apply a set of skills known to teachers and students as ELA standards.

When you think about what students need to truly be able to apply across content areas and throughout life, you should think about high cognitive literacy tasks. Every Common Core State Standard is more than just an ELA standard; each standard represents a life skill that students must be able to implement independently.

This looks different for each content area as well as each situation in life. In social studies, students need to apply thinking about why a text was written, who wrote the text, is the information objective or subjective, and what do others say about the same topic? When students read like historians, they need to be able to understand and evaluate sequence of events, compare and contrast key events, and analyze the cause and effect relationship among and between events in history.

For science, students need to be able to evaluate claims about the world around them and weigh those claims against other works in the field or against recreating the work in order to test the reliability and validity of the claim. When students read like scientists, they need to be able to recognize processes, interpret data, generate and test hypotheses, and analyze cause and effect relationships among and between natural, chemical, and tested situations.

In mathematics, students need to be able to problem-solve when presented with relevant and irrelevant information and explain how they got the answer as well as support why it works. When students read like mathematicians, they need to question variables, explore multiple possibilities to the same answers, and interpret and explain data.

This application and utilization of ELA standards (or skills) continues throughout life. Students will become adults in a world full of scandal, as well as unknown, misrepresented, and misled information that they will need to work through, and only high cognitive thinking of the presentation of information (literacy) will help them be critical consumers and creators. For example, if your air-conditioning goes out, you should research why and weigh the cost of fixing it versus replacing it. Then if you choose to replace it, you will need to research different units, companies, and manufacturers' warranties. You will also want to get references and interview the companies all before you make your well-informed decision. A lot of money is on the line that only high cognitive thinking can help you spend productively.

Some people say they do not read, but everyone reads. Perhaps you do not see the presentation of information all around you as reading. Maybe you only see reading contained within a novel. Reading is when you look at e-mails, text messages, surf the Internet, drive, shop, talk, listen, and observe. Reading is literacy, and literacy is a form of presented information. Okay, now that you know you are a reader, let's dive into high cognitive literacy tasks that will move your students closer to mastering the Common Core State Standards (CCSS) for English/Language Arts (ELA).

So far, you have learned three reading closely strategies to help students master Reading Informational Text Standards 1, 2, 3, and 5 of the CCSS. In this chapter, you will explore techniques to get students to master Reading Informational and Literary Text Standards 6, 8, and 9 of the CCSS. This is where your journey begins.

PLANNING FOR HIGH COGNITIVE TASKS

No matter what you read in a professional text, you should always refer back to your standards. Every decision you make should be based on your standards. In this case, you are learning with the CCSS for ELA grade 6; however, the strategies discussed throughout this text are applicable for any set of standards.

In the following example, it is the start of third quarter, and you are ready to move into providing direct instruction with meaningful practice around a group of standards (RI.6.6, RL.6.6, RI.6.8, RI.6.9, and RL.6.9—see http://www.corestandards.org/ for additional information on the standards). Also, keep in mind the different ways to use texts. For instance, think about using previous text to introduce each strategy to teach the standards. Consider using short excerpts for collaborative practice, or take into account the use of longer, more complex pieces of text for independent practice. This progression will chunk the learning into digestible bites and allow students to truly master the grade level expectations.

By reusing text students have already experienced, you will spend less time looking for supplemental text, students will already be familiar with the content and truly be able to focus on the semantics and syntax, and you will spend less time planning. Let's refer back to the first text, "Bacteria: The Good, the Bad, and the Stinky" by Joy Masoff in *Read-Aloud Anthology* by Janet Allen and Patrick Daley (2004), as an example for rereading familiar text with a new purpose. Remember, whatever you are going to plan for students to do, you must experience it first.

Reread the previously read text, and determine the point of view. The point of view is how the author chooses to communicate. Point of view is difficult for students to explain, but they are expected to be able to do this by the end of sixth grade. There are four basic types of point of view: first person with the use of personal pronouns such as *I*, second person addressing the reader with the use of *you*, third person limited told by a narrator who only knows the main character's thinking but is aware of others' actions, and third person omniscient also told by a narrator, but one who knows everything thought about every character; both use pronouns that refer to someone, such as *he*, *she*, or a name.

In the text mentioned in chapter 2, the author's point of view is second person. For example, the author specifically addresses the reader with the use of the word *your*, "your hands." Questions you want to pose to groups during this reread are:

- What point of view is this text written in and how do you know?
- Why does the author choose this point of view?
- What would happen if you changed the point of view to a personal narrative or third person?

In addition, standard 6 asks students to be able to address the author's purpose. This is why a text is written. Generally, there are four basic reasons authors write: to inform, to persuade, to entertain, or to explain. Students need to be able to connect the perspective and purpose in order to support word choices that are objective or subjective.

Looking into the same text, paragraph 4 reads, "Most bacteria are totally cool little microbes (another name for microorganisms)." So during this reread, students can have discussion around questions that drive the author's purpose, such as

- What is the author's purpose for writing this text and how do you know?
- What would happen if you changed every positive word in paragraph 4 to a negative word? Does this change the author's purpose?

This leads directly into standard 8; students must evaluate the information authors present and determine whether it is valid or invalid, objective or subjective, and if the claims properly support the argument with sufficient evidence. Ask yourself if the details provided are statements of facts or interpretations or opinions. Is the source a primary or secondary source? Is the information only provided from one perspective? There are signal words you can teach students to look for, such as *should* or *appropriate*, that represent vague, immeasurable terms. Words like *right* or *wrong* represent moral terms. Does the author use words of judgment such as *fair*, *deserves*, or *earn*?

When your students reread for this purpose, ask them to think about the semantics (word choice). For example, paragraph 3 reads, "What do bacteria love to do most of all? Munch!" The author could have used several words to express this point, but chose those words, so ask students to think about why by using guiding questions, such as

- Is the author for or against the topic and how do you know?
- How many statements of facts versus opinions versus interpretations does the author use? Are those statements meant to support?
- What do other sources say about the topic?
- Can you triangulate the information?

Looking into bias (RI.8) and perspective (RI.6) requires students to recall skills from standard 4, which states students are able to study the semantics (word choice) in order to determine the relationship between words and meaning within the syntax (sentence structure). This directly impacts author's tone. Students should know to look for words used that imply a type of tone, such as *vibrant* for a positive tone, *arrogant* for a negative tone, *teasing* for a humorous tone, *somber* for a fearful tone, or *sincere* for a neutral tone.

Now you want to plan for students to reread for another purpose. Each purpose opens another way of looking at the same text. Paragraph 7 reads, "One of the main ways that bully bacteria are spread is through bad hygiene. Translation?" You know the author made specific word choices for this paragraph. Now you need your students to be cognizant of those choices. Plan for students to have discussion around the following questions:

- What words pop out at you and why?
- How do those words impact the interpretation of the text?
- Change the word(s) . . . How does it change the mood of the text?
- What is the tone of the text, and which words support that attitude?
- Is the author biased or unbiased, and what words support your conclusion?

Once students have analyzed all three texts separately in the ways explained, they are ready to place the texts side by side to compare and contrast each author's approach to the topic (RI.9). This requires them to weigh the information presented in each text on the same topic. The purpose is to prepare them to be critical of presented information and think about facts versus opinions, valid versus invalid, supported and valid evidence, and the context in which the information is presented. This truly prepares them to be active citizens because they will be able to analyze advertisements, commercials, political actions, as well as political speeches in order to make an informed decision during election times or in times of important purchases or life changes.

In order to compare and contrast the supplemental texts, consider the following example. Take a look back at the three different texts. Let's refer to the first text, "Bacteria: The Good, the Bad, and the Stinky" by Joy Masoff in *Read-Aloud Anthology* by Janet Allen and Patrick Daley (2004). Paragraph 2 reads, "One bacterium can divide into a million bacteria in half a day!" In the second text, *The Demon in the Freezer* by Richard Preston (2002), paragraph 1 reads, "Viruses are parasites that multiply inside the cells of their hosts, and they are the smallest life forms." The last text from www.eyewitnesstohistory.com, *The Black Death, 1348* (2001) reads, "The violence of this disease was such that the sick communicated it to the healthy who came near them, just as a fire catches anything dry or oily near it."

The key to pulling these three sentences out demonstrates the need to break the texts apart and determine which details agree and which details disagree. All three of these sentences are communicating a similar message about bacteria and viruses, but students do not tend to read with this critical eye. By the time they take all the text and work with this standard, they are also ready to address the content standard, "compare and contrast types of infectious agents that may infect the human body, including viruses, bacteria, fungi, and parasites" (CPALMS, 2012, SC.6.L.14.6). Have them work with a small group or with a partner to tackle questions that drive compare and contrast across multiple texts, such as

- How is the topic the same or different across all the texts?
- How is the author's purpose the same or different across all the texts?
- How is the author's tone the same or different across all the texts?
- Which details can be triangulated and which details will require inquiry in order to determine the accuracy of the interpretation?
- Find three additional resources to validate or invalidate the details of these three texts (record findings in your evidence log found in appendix H).
- Which author makes the most convincing claims about bacteria or viruses and why?

Learning is all about challenging your thinking and actions to the point where you change something, such as a thought, an opinion, or a way of doing or being. This is what teachers try to facilitate in their classroom every day. When the lightbulb goes off, or a student realizes something different or new, this is why you teach.

TEACHING FOR HIGH COGNITIVE TASKS

For this instructional example, you will take a look into Ms. Williams's sixth grade classroom again, but this time, she is using all three texts for students to think about critically. The purpose for participating in a fourth or fifth read is to plan for students to analyze the semantics and the impact on the syntax as well as the relationship between sentences and paragraphs, which results in high cognitive tasks. As you read, think about how the teacher facilitates this type of learning among the students. However, by this point, the interaction with the text needs to be mostly driven by students.

As you walk through Ms. Williams's classroom door, you will see students arranged in groups of three all over the room. The teacher assigns students to groups as they walk through the classroom door. She hands a playing card to each student. The numbers on the cards range from 2 to 9 and represent three out of the four suits (hearts, clubs, spades, diamonds). Each student has three texts in front of him/her: (1) "Bacteria: The Good, the Bad, and the Stinky" by Joy Masoff in *Read-Aloud Anthology* by Janet Allen and Patrick Daley (2004), (2) *The Demon in the Freezer* by Richard Preston (2002), and (3) *The Black Death, 1348* (2001).

"Okay. Okay. Each group has a graphic organizer to guide your analysis of the texts. You should each have the three texts we've used over the past six days out and ready to go. Look at the playing card you received as you walked through the class door today. All of you have the same number; that's how you know you're a group. However, you each have a different symbol. If you have the heart, then you are the facilitator of your group. You'll keep your group on task, focused, and on time, but you're still responsible for adding to the discussion," Ms. Williams states as she also draws the symbol (heart) and writes the role (facilitator) on the board.

"All right, if you have a diamond, then you're the recorder for your group. You need to capture your discussion on the graphic organizer, but you're also responsible for adding to the discussion. If you have a spade, then you're the presenter for your group. You'll be responsible for representing your group in the inner circle discussion once we come back together, but you're still responsible for adding to the discussion within your group," the teacher explains as she records the information on the board.

"Your group will have forty minutes total to go back into each text for another expert read. This time your focus needs to be around the word choice and sentence structure in terms of the guiding questions on your graphic organizer. Tomorrow we will hold an inner circle discussion with an outer circle review followed by a reflection and debrief.

"Independently, you'll start with 'Bacteria: The Good, the Bad, and the Stinky,' and I'll give you six minutes to complete an expert read. During your expert read, you'll need to circle descriptive words the author has chosen to use that imply perspective, tone, purpose, bias, and text structure, which all work together to impact the meaning. Then I'll signal you to move to the next text, *The Demon in the Freezer*, and you'll have three minutes to do the same thing with that text. I'll call switch texts one more time, and you'll read *The Black Death, 1348* for eleven minutes, completing the same task to close the dialogue.

"After the third article, I will call time and you'll move into working collaboratively to compare and contrast the word choice evidence using the guiding questions on the graphic organizer. You'll only have half your time left to complete this step and be prepared for tomorrow, so facilitators, please keep your group moving along. Now, I'd like a couple of students to reiterate today's expectations," Ms. Williams requests.

A few students' hands go up to volunteer. "We're going to reread each article and have a role and work together to fill in the graphic organizer," a student from the far back of the room says.

"Good, now someone from the front of the room," the teacher directs.

The same hands shoot up again, but the teacher calls on a young boy sitting to the far left in the front with his back to the door. "Chris?"

"Um, we'll read back over these stories and uh, help complete the worksheet so we can talk about it tomorrow."

"Great, let's do the first paragraph together of each text just to make sure we all have the same understanding," Ms. Williams suggests.

"Will someone read the first paragraph of the 'Bacteria' text out loud?"

"John, thank you."

John reads the entire first paragraph aloud while the rest follow along. "What words jump out at you that describe perspective, purpose, structure, and tone? Think back to the entire text from four days ago," inquires Ms. Williams.

"So it's written in second person explaining the good and the bad of bacteria, and so I focused on *cover*, *thrive*, and *belong*," Steven offers.

"Okay, Steven, so you told us the perspective and purpose and identified three words . . . why?"

"Oh, well, each of those words helps with the tone. So bacteria is not weak, but you know, serious," Steven explains.

"Let's keep that in mind and move to the next text," the teacher directs. "Volunteer to read?"

"Jessica?"

Jessica reads the entire first paragraph of the *Demon* text and then without prompting offers her thinking: "This one is written in third person, explaining the smallpox virus, but the words that help with the feeling are *entangled, victim, multiply, affinity, eradicated*, and . . . are those right?"

"What does the class think?"

Heads nod up and down all across the room. "So what do those words imply the tone is toward the topic?"

"Well, smallpox is powerful, but don't worry cause they've got it . . . you know under control," Jessica adds.

"So what do we know about both texts so far?" Ms. Williams asks.

"That bacteria and viruses spread quick?" Justice somewhat states but with a slight inflection of uncertainty.

"What do you all think?"

"I think they both can support spreading fast because of the words *thrive* and *multiply* and *belong* and *affinity*. They spread and love to be in humans," Zaria explains.

"I believe you all are on the right track. Let's read the first paragraph of the *Black Death* text and then we'll bring it all together," Ms. Williams suggests. "Volunteer to read?"

"James?"

James quickly reads the short paragraph and looks up at the teacher with a blank stare. "James, what are your thoughts?" Ms. Williams prompts.

"I don't know, I just read it," James retorts.

"Well, part of reading is thinking. Take a minute and reread it to yourself. I'm going to come back to you for perspective and purpose. Chris, what word choice supports the tone?"

"I'm seein' *unleashing a rampage* and *un-prec-e-dent-ed*. They make it sound really bad."

"What would happen to the tone if the author would have said *it spread across Europe quickly*?"

"That don't sound that bad," Devon yells out.

"Good. So his words make a very specific impact on the reader," the teachers points out. "James, now what are you thinking?"

"It is third person and it tells me about the Black Death," James offers.

"That's a solid starting point for us. Now let's look at the graphic organizer or the 'worksheet,' as Chris referred to it. We'll take the information offered during our discussion and write into the graphic organizer. I'll need your help to fully complete it." Table 5.1 is a sample graphic organizer filled in for your reference; the blank graphic organizer is available in appendix I. Ms. Williams works with the students to recall the discussion and fill out the pieces of the graphic organizer.

"Great work. Now, remember we are a community of learners, so even if you finish reading before I call switch, we've committed to staying quiet while everyone finishes. Thumbs up if you are clear on our goals for today." Ms. Williams waits until all thumbs go up around the room. It takes a minute, but eventually they all are up. "Let's get started, and I'll be around to guide you if your group needs it once we move from reading to collaborating."

She walks around the room while the students reread the first article. They are circling words or phrases. It is very important to move about when students are working, because it sends an unspoken message that what they are doing is very important. "Switch texts!"

Even as the students reread the second text, she is still moving around. She stops at a few desks to observe what students are circling for evidence. This is crucial because it serves as an informal check for understanding. If the teacher notices students are not on the right track, then she can reteach or have them work a little more together. "Last text!"

The third text is the longest and most difficult, so it is extremely important for the teacher to circulate during the final reread. Some students will need to be encouraged to keep going. Some students may need to be redirected or refocused. The most important thing to remember is to circulate, circulate, and circulate!

"Okay, okay. Let's bring it back together. Now, you will have some time to work with your group to fill in the graphic organizer. Remember this will prepare you for inner and outer discussion. Are there any questions?" Ms. Williams asks.

Heads go in and rear ends go up as students start the collaboration process of filling in the graphic organizer. The teacher is of course moving around the room ready to challenge thinking or redirect if she needs to do so. Students will be able to use this completed graphic organizer as one more tool for writing their final compare and contrast piece at the end of the unit of instruction on infectious agents.

Table 5.1. Sample Lesson for Analyzing Craft and Structure

Text	Structure	Point of View	Purpose	Tone
"Bacteria: The Good, the Bad, and the Stinky" by Joy Masoff in Read-Aloud Anthology by Janet Allen and Patrick Daley (2004)	Compare and contrast Evidence: instead, most, other, then there are, different, like	second person Evidence: bacteria, they, you, your	define, describe and inform Evidence: bacteria are, such as, like the ones	Playfully serious Evidence: a snap, lurking, munch, totally cool, geeky, bully
Excerpt from *The Demon in the Freezer* by Richard Preston (2002)	time order Evidence: first became, began, after, then, since	third person Evidence: smallpox, human, person, people, victim	define, describe and explain Evidence: smallpox is, two forms	Seriously dangerous Evidence: explosively contagious, splitting is extraordinary, develop extreme
The Black Death, 1348 (2001)	cause & effect Evidence: cause, symptoms, by so doing, because, thus	third person Evidence: black death, victims, men, women, they	define, describe and explain Evidence: three interrelated forms, symptoms	Extremely dangerous Evidence: inevitable death, violence of this disease

FINAL THOUGHT

Consequently, students have received direct instruction in tone, mood, purpose, point of view, perspective and text structure prior to applying this knowledge across three texts. So check for understanding first. It is not enough for students to simply read text one time. Good readers often reexamine text to peel away the layers of meaning that can be missed with a simple run over. Think about your favorite book or movie that you have read or watched several times. There are a lot of reasons why you get a little more each time. One reason is your brain already has an understanding of what will happen, so it looks for details missed that may have hinted or suggested the ending. Another reason is your brain grows and stretches with every experience, which puts you in a different mind-set each time you venture back to the book or movie. Finally, the time of your life can impact the meaning, the depth, and the understanding that you walk away with from a movie or book.

Reading is like art in the fact that it is abstract and meaning is given by the person interacting with the text. Your background, experience, knowledge, and emotional mind-set all impact your interaction with literacy. This is why events, situations, poems, music, or art evoke different interpretations for every observer, including the creator or author.

Remember to start this process with high interest, as well as complex, grade-level-appropriate text in order to get your students to buy into the process. If you believe they can, then they will believe they can, but if you do not believe they are capable, then they will not believe they are capable. Set the expectations, provide the supports and scaffolds, and watch your students rise to the high cognitive tasks with full engagement and unthinkable success!

Chapter Six

Multiple Interactions with Literary Texts

Many times teachers learn great strategies or instructional practices from workshops, trainings, or professional texts, but they attempt to adopt rather than adapt, or they have a difficult time visualizing how those strategies or practices transfer to other situations. This chapter will guide you through that thinking. You will discover how to use each approach with poems, fables, narratives, and classic novels, as well as make the practices your own.

To begin, you will take a look at the difference between reading informational standards versus reading literary standards versus the end in mind, the College and Career Readiness Anchor Standards for Reading (CCR).

The first reading standard is exactly the same for informational and literary. What is important here is the standard development or progression that happens vertically. If you look at the sixth grade standard, the key words are *cite evidence, analysis of explicit meaning*, and *inferences*. However, if you travel back two grade levels to fourth grade, then you will notice *evidence* is replaced with *details and examples* and *cite* is replaced with *refer*. On the other hand, if you move back to fifth grade, you will notice *refer* becomes *quote* and *details and examples* becomes *the text*. Is there a difference between these words? This educator and author believes there is a slight difference that works to prepare students for the end in mind, CCR:

- *Refer*—to regard a source or make mention of the source without specifically stating the information from the source.
- *Quote*—to copy the text verbatim in order to support thinking during discussion or writing from a source.

- *Cite*—to refer to a source and provide textual evidence in your own words in order to support thinking during text-based discussions or writing to learn.

The second standard is very similar with the exception of the word *theme* added to the literary standard. Again if you track the progression, you will notice two grades back from sixth, it says students will determine the main idea of a text. However, one grade level back, it says students will determine main ideas within a text. Other key words that are a part of this standard are *central idea, central theme, details,* and *summary*. The difference here is that in literary text there is a main point and usually a theme, which is the life lesson that is learned as result of the characters and plot development.

Standard 3 has some similarities, but the vocabulary is different due to the genre. For example in informational text at the sixth grade level, students are looking at how key individuals, events, and ideas are developed over the length of the text, whereas in literary text, students look at how a character grows as the plot develops over the length of text. If you peek two grades back, you will notice students only look at one aspect and track the development, and one grade back, they compare and contrast two aspects over the course of the text. This is to get them to think critically about the why in addition to the how in the long run.

The difference between the informational and literary standard 4 is in the second part of the standard. In literary text, students look at how word choice impacts meaning and tone, but with informational text, students look at technical meanings, how words are used with that specific topic or content. Key words in this standard are *determine word meaning, figurative,* and *connotative*. These differences change through the progression of the standard and move from specific types of language to a more vague understanding of context clues, affixes, connotative and denotative meaning, and figurative language as well as how they the impact the meaning and tone of the text.

Informational standard 5 moves students from describing the overall text structures to comparing and contrasting text structures of multiple texts to determining how parts of a text fit into the overall text structure. Similarly, the literary standard takes students from identifying the story elements and how they build on top of each other to comparing and contrasting literary elements for different type of literary texts to how the overall structure impacts the theme or idea of the text.

At first glance, the progression of standard 6 appears as though the skill gets easier. Students move from comparing and contrasting primary and secondary accounts across texts to analyzing point of view on the same topic across multiple texts to determining point of view at the sixth grade level. However, purpose is added as well as how the author or narrator uses the details of the text to convey point of view or purpose. This is to prepare students for distinguishing how authors present their position through the use of point of view or purpose in the next grade. Every year the standards build to move students toward CCR.

Standard 7 pushes teachers to think beyond printed text, but into multiple literacies of a twenty-first-century world full of digital natives. Students need to be able to compare and contrast digital literacy or text such as video and audio with printed text, and they need to think about how this type of literacy adds to the understanding of the topic. If teachers leave out digital literacy or opportunities to apply literacy skills to the digital world, then students will not be fully prepared to thrive in a future unknown.

Literary does not have an eighth standard; however, informational does. This standard truly shifts the cognitive load through the progression as students go from explaining argument and claims to tracing and evaluating arguments and claims in order to determine if the argument and claim is reasonably supported or not.

The progression of the ninth standard moves students from using an array of information on the same topic from multiple texts to write or talk about to comparing and contrasting how one author presents information versus how another presents information on the same topic within informational text. Similarly, for literary text students compare and contrast how different genres address similar themes.

By knowing the differences between literary standards and informational standards, you can plan to adapt any strategy you learn for students to use when they need to analyze text and dig deeper into the meaning behind, between, and beyond the words written on the page.

CHANGE PERSPECTIVE WITH LITERARY

Remember the purpose of this strategy is to open the minds of students to look at text differently in order for true learning to take place. Literary text is amazing because it serves many purposes, such as capturing historical events, teaching valuable life lessons (themes), communicating values and beliefs from throughout the decades, and providing entertainment or comfort on a rainy day or a day of relaxation on the beach.

All of these purposes will help drive the different perspectives you have available to choose from, as well as the structural elements of literary text (plot, character, resolution, conflict, and setting). Table 6.1 provides you with some suggestions for perspective reading for literary text, but these are not the only choices.

To use this approach with literary text, you will go through the same planning process as you did in chapter 2 with informational text. What standards do you want your students to know, understand, and do? How will you assess if they know it, understand it, and can apply it? What materials or resources will you need, what activities or assignments will you design, and what explicit instruction will you provide?

Most content area teachers do not use literary text, which is a missed opportunity because there are literary texts for almost any and all topics. Appendix J offers a few topics and titles as examples for using literary text in content classes, but for even more titles categorized by topic, you can read *Read, Discuss, and Learn: Using Literacy Groups to Student Advantage* by Lisa Fisher (2010). One way for content area teachers to pick literature connected to their topic (standards) is to communicate with their language arts teacher or the media/library specialist. S/he will be able to recommend some great titles.

Table 6.1. Optional Reading Closely Perspectives for Literary Text

Perspective A	Perspective B
Antagonist	Protagonist
Says/Thinks	Does/Acts
Direct Characterization	Indirect Characterization
Choices	Consequences
Survivor	Deserter

The literary piece will personalize the content. For example, the sixth grade teacher working on the four-week unit of instruction around the infectious agent standard can have her students read *Fever 1793* by Laurie Halse Anderson (2000) or *Code Orange* by Caroline Cooney (2005). The students can read these titles outside of class but use the knowledge that they gain to add to the discussion in class around the factual content. If you ask students to take on the role of detective and find evidence that may lead to a spread of bacteria or viruses, then just in the first five pages of *Fever 1793*, the main character is bitten by a mosquito and handles a dead mouse, which should spark discussion from students based on their learning around the way bacteria and viruses spread.

The multiple reading opportunities for this text can come when you ask them to revisit a page or two with a scientist's lens. For example, during the expert read partner A can interact with the text for how yellow fever affected setting and partner B can interact with the text for how yellow fever affected characters' actions.

The power in this strategy is that you believe in the process and use it for the right purpose, with the right text, and at the right moments. The strategy empowers students to open their minds and then discuss the similarities and differences of their perspective with a partner. The desired effect is that students enjoy reading to learn and the challenge of critical analysis when they interact with complex text multiple times.

Ultimately, the end in mind is to move students toward choosing the perspectives connected to the learning target after the cold read and then leading the class discussion, which moves them toward truly demonstrating mastery of standard 10, "read and comprehend complex literary and informational texts independently and proficiently" (College and Career Readiness Anchor Standards for Reading, p. 35).

PREVIEW/REVIEW WITH LITERARY

This strategy is specifically designed for informational text; however, the approach can be used with different forms of literary texts, such as dramas and stories. Again, the main purpose for using this approach is to help students extract evidence from the text and build a table of contents in the margin aligned to the structure in order to support connections and distinctions within, among, and between individuals, events, and ideas in reference to the learning target. This should lead to noting relevant and irrelevant information provided. The same process for planning discussed under *Change Perspective* holds value for this approach too.

This is a difficult approach to learn because it requires students to annotate in the margins. It is best if you start with summarizing in the margins before you have them identify evidence to support relationships or comparisons of character, plot, and setting. When you have students practice summarizing in the margins to create a table of contents, provide them with some guidance. Tell them to start with who, what, when, and where. Then move them into noting in the margin the subject and action. Eventually, you want them jotting down points from each section of the drama or story that drives the central idea or theme and shows causal relationships between character and plot.

To use this approach with literary text, you will go through the same planning process as you did in chapter 3 with informational text. What standards do you want your students to know, understand, and do? How will you assess if they know it, understand it, and can apply it? What materials or resources will you need, what activities or assignments will you design, and what explicit instruction will you provide?

Think about the infectious agent standard used throughout this book. If you use *Fever 1793* by Laurie Halse Anderson (2000) for this approach too, then you will have students revisit sections of the novel in order to build their understanding of the content standard and allow them to analyze text to build their understanding of and application of life skills.

The multiple reading opportunities for this text can come when you ask students to revisit a page or two with a scientist's lens and compare and contrast the text to other information they have read during this unit of instruction. So students will create a table of contents using sticky notes for evidence of similarities and differences of how yellow fever spread, affected humans, and impacted life versus other viruses they've read about so far. Every layer of literacy you set students up to interact with will only add to their processing and expand their learning experiences.

The strength of using this approach will only exist if you truly believe in the process and use it with intentional teaching for intentional learning. The approach inspires students to see the importance of content everywhere around them and then discuss the similarities and differences between the forms of literacy presenting the content. The desired effect is that students become lifelong learners and think critically about the information presented all around them, even in dramas and stories.

Similarly to change perspective, the end in mind is to move students toward choosing the information to extract from the text connected to the learning target after the cold read and then lead peer discussion, which moves students toward mastery of CCR Anchor Standard 10 for Reading.

STRATEGIC APPROACH WITH LITERARY

Remember this is the most complex strategy and requires students to text mark and then categorize their text marking so they can draw a final conclusion with textual evidence. Recall the main purpose for this approach is to help students interact with a text multiple times to prepare for supporting an argument that demonstrates connections and distinctions within, among, and between the central idea and details in reference to the learning target. The same process for planning discussed under change perspective and preview/review is needed for this approach too.

This is a difficult approach to learn because it requires students to categorize text markings (or text coding). For this approach, you will start with letting the students know what the text structure is after the cold read. Literary texts are organized using literary elements (characters, setting, problem/solution, and plot). Then provide them with the category choices for grouping the text markings. Remember students do one cold read and two expert reads with this approach.

To use this approach with literary text, you will go through the same planning process as you did in chapter 4 with informational text. What standards do you want your students to know, understand, and do? How will you assess if they know it, understand it, and can apply it? What materials or resources will you need, what activities or assignments will you design, and what explicit instruction will you provide? This is continuously reiterated throughout this text because it is the most intentional way to plan for intentional teaching that results in intentional learning.

To help you make connections, go back to the same science standard on infectious agents referenced throughout this book, and refer back to the novel *Fever 1793* by Laurie Halse Anderson (2000) for this approach too. You will have students revisit sections of the novel in order to refine their understanding of the content standard and allow them to analyze text to expand their application of embedded ELA standards.

Providing students with multiple opportunities to read the same text over and over again as a content expert will allow them to truly analyze down to the word choice level in order to validate or invalidate the use of details that support the central idea or central theme. So students will reread preidentified parts of the text in order to text mark for the main character's (Matilda) actions, thoughts, or conversations (cause) and response of others, change in setting or plot, or change for/in Matilda (effect).

Then students will go back to those text markings to read again and categorize their thinking into preestablished labels (ignorance, encounters, or living conditions). This will allow students to see literary text as a source for support during discussions, writing to sources, or answering questions. Every interaction of text students experience will only expand their ability for learning to take place.

Of course, it does not matter how much the data proves this reading closely approach works if you do not believe in it or present it to students as if it is something they have to do. The strength of using this approach is solely in your instructional ability to sell it like you are trying to sell someone oceanfront property in Colorado. The desired effect is that students become critical readers and thinkers about the information presented all around them, even in dramas and stories.

Similarly to change perspective and preview/review, the end in mind is to move students toward choosing the overall text structure connected to the learning target after the cold read and then choosing the categories connected to the overall idea after the first expert read, which moves students toward mastery of CCR Anchor Standard 10 for Reading.

TEACHING LITERARY ANALYSIS WITH CLOSE AND CAREFUL READING

Let's recap where you have been so far with this unit of instruction. You started by identifying your content standard to teach—"compare and contrast types of infectious agents that may infect the human body, including viruses, bacteria, fungi, and parasites" (CPALMS, 2012, SC.6.L.14.6). Then, you created a scale so students can track their progression toward learning the standard. Next, you designed your end in mind, students will write a compare and contrast research paper on infectious agents using the multiple literacies as evidence throughout their paper, and you designed a rubric to grade the assessment task.

Following the end in mind, you selected materials and resources, such as articles, videos, sections of the textbook, labs, and literary text. Afterward, you mapped out your day-to-day instruction. Day 1, you kicked off the unit of instruction with a playfully serious article, "Bacteria: The Good, the Bad, and the Stinky" by Joy Masoff in *Read-Aloud Anthology* by Janet Allen and Patrick Daley (2004) with embedded literacy strategies (reading closely with change perspective). Day 2, you had students watch a short video on bacteria and read a short section in their textbook on bacteria and compare and contrast the three sources (article, video, and textbook).

The next day, you had students interact with text again, *The Demon in the Freezer* by Richard Preston (2002), to kick off the next part of the standard with embedded literacy (using reading closely preview/review). Day 4, you had students watch another quick clip on viruses and read a section in their textbook on viruses and compare and contrast the three sources.

The last day of week 1, you had students watch a quick video on the plague and interact with vocabulary through a word splash, which included discussions and connections to what they have learned so far. Now on day 6, students are fully ready to interact with a complex text, *The Black Death* from EyeWitness to History (2001), using a reading closely strategy, *Strategic Approach*. Then, you asked students to work in groups to create a T-chart between bacteria and viruses and cite evidence from any source they have interacted with so far to support their comparisons.

On the seventh day in the unit of instruction, you had students interact with an article about fungi, and then the following day compare and contrast the information from the article to the information presented in the textbook. Thursday of week 2, you started class with a picture of a parasite and had students generate an observation report without talking. Afterward, they switched reports without talking and wrote comments and questions to their partner. This was followed by a quick video on parasites and discussion about the information presented digitally versus visually through the picture. On Friday, students read a short article on parasites and the section in their textbook to add or change their observation report on parasites.

By week 3, students have many tools to assist them to write their final paper, but you are not done yet. This is where you step back into Ms. Williams's sixth grade science classroom, where students are reading *Fever 1793* by Laurie Halse Anderson (2000) at home and coming to class ready for discussion and hands-on labs for the last two weeks of this unit of instruction.

It is Monday, and students have a look of rest and tolerance on their faces. They were given the book on Friday and asked to read the first five pages. Students enter the room, and they are asked to reach into a mostly closed bucket to pull out one item. The items vary from toy rats to toy snakes to wadded-up napkins to a pencil. However, as they handle the item and look at it, they notice something on their hand. Ms. Williams acts as if there is nothing wrong. "Good morning, class. Thank you for picking up your item from the bucket. Please take your seats and take out your observation report. Record your observations about your item and how it is connected to the information you read last night in *Fever 1793* and compare your observations to what you have learned through this unit of instruction on infectious agents. Be prepared to share in five minutes."

The students are in several different places in this process. Some students are attempting to clean their hands, some students are rotating their item around, and some students start writing right away. The teacher is moving around the room taking roll and directing students to start writing. She assures them they will get cleaned up. "That's time, so let's share our thinking."

Students turn to their shoulder partner and discuss their writings. Conversation booms from every direction. Students are excited and extremely interested because they were not sure exactly what was going to happen next. Ms. Williams has their attention! "Sara, will you share your thinking?"

"I pulled a fake bug out of the bucket," she says as she holds it up high and turns in her seat to show everyone. "Okay, so this is what I wrote—*This bug is like the mosquito that bit Matilda describe on page 2 in* Fever *1793. From reading about the plague, I know bugs can carry infectious agents that can be transferred to us and cause us to be sick. But the more I touched this fake bug, the more I got stuff on my hand; I think it's glitter. It doesn't come off easily. I wonder if it is just as hard to get rid of infectious agents?*"

"Thank you for sharing your thinking, Sara. Challenger and questioner?" Ms. Williams poses to the group. "Zach."

"Are you sayin' she's goin' get sick from that mosquito bite?" Zach asks.

"Well, the book is called *Fever*, so it could happen," Sara answers.

"You're assuming all mosquitoes or bugs carry infectious agents from just a few articles," April chimes into the discussion.

"Okay, so I didn't think about if it's all bugs, but aren't bugs nasty?" Sara asks.

"Let's hold off on that for a minute, and I've captured that question over here on our inquiry chart. I'd like at least one more person to share," Ms. Williams encourages. "Oh, Justin, you could not have pulled a better item, so will you share?"

"Sure." He swings his item, a rat, around his head for everyone to see and laughs at his amusement. "I pulled this rubber rat. This reminds me of the mouse Matilda picked up and threw outside on page 4, and I was thinking that as this glitter got on my hands, that could be the germs from the dead mouse. This makes me think Matilda touching that dead mouse is how she gets the fever."

"Questions or challenges?"

"Why's everyone thinking Matilda gets sick?" Devon asks.

"We're not assuming, we're predicting based on what's happened so far and what the title says," Justin answers.

"Does every animal have bacteria, or just dead ones, or just you know, like rats and stuff?" Melissa wonders.

"Great question, Melissa, let's put that on our inquiry chart," Ms. Williams interjects. "We are not done yet. Everyone rub your hands together as fast as you can. What do you notice?"

"The glitter is falling off," a student calls from the back of the room.

"Great! Do you think the same thing happens to microbacteria or germs on your hands?"

"Yeah," another student yells out.

"What do you notice about everywhere you touched before you rubbed your hands together?"

"Aw, man, it's all over my book bag!"

"It's on my jeans."

"Some got on my desk."

"Great. Now, this side of the room, go run your hands under water without soap and dry them with a paper towel. The other side of the room, go to the other sink and wash your hands with the antibacterial soap and dry them with a paper towel. Then pair up with someone from the opposite group and be prepared to share out your observations," Ms. Williams directs.

The students join up and start discussing their observations. "Now join up with another pair so you have four in your group." They begin to have conflicting observations. "What do you notice?"

"Well, I used soap, but I still have some glitter on my hands," Ryan says.

"I didn't use soap, and it looks like all the glitter is off," Sabrina shares.

"Will you both demonstrate how you washed your hands?" Ms. Williams asks.

When the students act out how they washed their hands, lightbulbs go off around the room. Conversation bursts at the seam. "Tell me what you are all noticing."

"Well, you can't just put your hands under running water and move them back and forth, even with soap pumped into your hands. You gotta rub, like we did before we went to the water," Sara notices.

"So what can we learn from this little experiment?" Ms. Williams questions.

"Germs spread everywhere," Miaya shares.

"You don't even know you're spreading them," Zach adds.

"You gotta wash your hands after touching something *iffy*, like the bacteria article talks about after you use the bathroom," Jenn says.

"Now we're thinking. Will everyone return to your seats and go back into your observation reports? Record inferences or conclusions you can make based on your observations, and record questions you wonder about due to this experience. For homework, I'd like you to do a cold read of pages 6 to 23." Ms. Williams wraps up the class.

The next day, students come into the class anticipating something after yesterday's excitement. On the whiteboard, students are directed to answer a question in their observation reports: *What do people say or do after sickness is mentioned in* Fever 1793? *Cite evidence from pages 6–23 to support your thinking.* After about five minutes, students share their thinking with a partner as the teacher walks around and listens. Then they participate in a lab that requires them to hypothesize the amount of bacteria on certain surfaces (doorknobs, countertops, desks, etc.). Once each pair has their hypotheses, the teacher challenges students to explain the why behind their hypotheses. Next, they go to the microscope to examine slabs of bacteria taken from different places to validate or negate their hypotheses. Finally, they reflect about their research in their observation reports.

"All right, class. Tonight I want you to do a cold read of pages 24–45. I'll see you back here tomorrow to stretch your minds a little bit further," Ms. Williams challenges.

In the middle of the week, the students arrive to a question on the board: *What is Mother's reaction each time death is mentioned?* The students start talking and the teacher quickly hears, "I don't know." "I wasn't reading for that."

"Perfect. So each of you is given a chart. That chart has four columns. In the first column, you will see the page number and paragraphs referenced. In the second column, you will see a quote pulled from the identified page. In the third column, you must explain what the reaction is of the person/people hearing about the death, and in the last column, you must provide evidence to support your interpretation. Let's do one together," Ms. Williams explains.

"Turn to page 10. Do an expert read of just that page, but as you read, think about the question written on the board that you were not sure about when you first arrived." The students reread page 10 quietly to themselves.

"The second paragraph is quoted in the second column. What is your interpretation?"

"The mother seems mad," Sergio offers.

"How do you know this, Sergio?"

"The sentences when she speaks are short and to the point."

"What else?" the teacher probes.

"I think she's scared cause she changes the subject," Josh shares.

"What do you mean?"

"Well, Eliza and Matilda say that Polly might be sick, and her mom starts asking about the grandfather."

"Excellent, so in the evidence column, you will record words and phrases the author chose to use to impact meaning and tone. I'll walk around if you get stuck or need some coaching," Ms. Williams reminds the class. "Let's get to work."

Students are not rereading everything. The teacher has preidentified several places in the text to conduct an expert read with the guiding question driving decisions made when organizing details from the text. This takes most of the class period, and the students share out a few at the end. Tomorrow, students will examine how the human population responds to infectious agents spreading among society as well as how the human population responds to the vaccinations. The last day of the four-week unit will be for students to organize their thoughts and write their final compare and contrast paper. They will have to finish it over the weekend and turn it in on Monday.

The process students experienced demonstrates the importance of multiple forms of literacies, which good readers interact with multiples times and in several ways. Reading closely is not just a strategy; it is a way of interacting with text, which teaches students how to think. Does it take time? You bet it does, but the payout is inspiring students to be lifelong learners who think critically about the world around them in order to solve problems and make decisions.

FINAL THOUGHT

You are probably thinking, this is ludicrous; you do not spend this much time on one standard! So how much time do you spend, and what type of learners do you produce? This text is about challenging the traditional surface, "race to the top" teaching just to get through everything, and instead slow down, dig deeper, and inspire lifelong learners who are capable of thinking beyond the classroom.

You have read about a unit of instruction that unfolded with each turn of the page, but most importantly, you have read and learned about how to get your students to interact with text multiple times in order to stretch their mind, challenge their thinking, and support their learning with the use of reading closely strategies and intentional planning and teaching that help students learn.

Now, all you have to do is pull out your standards and get started with creating challenging lessons that push students' thinking in memorable ways for life. Remember that multiple interactions with text are your friend for helping students challenge their thinking, deepen their understanding, and build their desire for lifelong learning, so you are not telling them what to think, but empowering them with how to think. Good luck and do not be afraid to reach out for help in the planning and teaching process!

Appendix A
*Reading Closely:
Change Perspective Planning Template*

Standards:

1. _____

2. _____

3. _____

Lesson Essential Question/Learning Target:

1. _____

Assessment (formative/summative):

1. _____

Front-Load Vocabulary: *Direct students to locate and circle the words as you discuss them.*

1. _____

2. _____

3. _____

4. _____

5. _____

Cold Read—(Time to read: _____)

1. Number your paragraphs!

2. Read the text independently and think about the *who is, what is, when, where,* or *topic* and *what the author wants you to know about the topic.*

Partner Discussion: Have students turn to a shoulder partner and share their literal understanding of the text. Then share out whole class.

Expert Read—(Time to read: _____)

1. Give partners a different reading perspective:

   a. _____

   b. _____

2. Have them highlight in different colors the perspective they are assigned/choose.

Partner Discussion: Have students turn to a shoulder partner and share their highlighted perspective and why. Then share out whole class.

Ticket Out the Door:

1. _____

Appendix B
3–12 Reading Closely Sample Lessons

Grade 3 Lesson Plan: *Achoo!*
Retrieved from http://www.superteacherworksheets.com/reading-comp/
 4th-achoo_WBDRT.pdf
Created by Andrea Altman, Elementary Literacy Leader

Learning Target	LACC.3.1.1.1—Ask and answer questions to demonstrate understanding of a text, referring explicitly to the text as the basis for answers. LACC.3.1.1.2—Determine the main idea of a text; recount the key details and explain how they support the main idea. LACC.3.1.1.3—Describe the relationship between a series of historical events, scientific ideas or concepts, or steps in technical procedures in a text, using language that pertains to time, sequence, and cause/effect. LACC.3.1.2.6—Distinguish own point of view from that of the author of a text.

Front-Load	1. Number your paragraphs.
	2. Vocabulary
	    invade—to enter like an enemy (par. 2, sent. 4)
	    irritate—annoy (par. 4, sent. 3)
	    reflex—involuntary response to stimuli (par. 1, sent. 2)
	    bacteria—organism that can make you sick (par. 1, sent. 4)

Cold Read	Students read while thinking about: • What is the topic? • What does the author want me to know about the topic? Students discuss with a partner. Then the teacher asks students to share as a class. Teacher records the information on chart paper and clarifies any misconceptions.

Expert Read	Change perspective—students highlight for ONE perspective. (Determine who reads for which perspective by counting off or splitting the room in half.) - Read for causes of sneezing - Read for effects of sneezing Model using paragraph 5. Students read. Students share with a partner when they are done reading and compare their findings. Then, share out as a group. Record statements on chart paper. Clarify misconceptions if needed.
Answer Questions	Answer text-based questions. Question 1—Teacher model Question 2—You do together Question 3—Independent Discuss answers to questions and clarify misconceptions.
Ticket Out the Door	Answer the question *What are two reasons people sneeze?* Use evidence from the text to support your answer. Rubric - 3 points—identify two reasons and supply text evidence for each - 2 points—identify two reasons and supply text evidence for one reason - 1 point—identify two reasons without text evidence for support - 0 points—incorrectly identifies reasons for sneezing

Appendix B

Grade 6 Lesson Plan: *Why the Hare Runs Away Africa* (*Ewe*)
Retrieved from *Favorite Folktales from Around the World* edited by Jane Yolen
Created by Leslie Frick, Middle School Language Arts Teacher

Standard: CCSS.RL.6.1.1, CCSS.RL.6.1.2, CCSS.RL.6.1.3

Before Reading – Use 10 minutes here.

Learning Target: Students will be able to identify perspectives in order to deepen their ability to comprehend folktales.

Understand – Student will know what the text is (Why the Hare Runs Away) and how the text is connected to the theme (Tricksters, Rogues, and Cheats)

Know – Students will understand key words the author uses –

    Hoe – paragraph 4

    Extracted – paragraph 7

    Lagoon – paragraph 8

    Calabash – paragraph 9

    Slake – paragraph 8

    Interference – paragraph 12

    dummy-image – paragraph 15

    birdlime – paragraph 15

    saluted – paragraph 18

    accursed – paragraph 25

Connection: Tell students how folktales teach a lesson so many of them can be read in a similar way.

During Reading –

Appendix B

Cold Read: Give students 15 minutes to read the text.

- Make sure students have a literal understanding:
- Then ask students to fill in the Folk Tale Matrix (or ask students Who is in the text? What happens in the text? How does the text end? Where does the story take place?)

Expert Reading: Give students 15 minutes to reread the text.

- Students will choose one perspective to highlight/underline during the second read.
    - Read to identify Good Behavior Choices OR
    - Read to identify Bad Behavior Choices
- Then have each student pair up with the opposite perspective and share their information they extracted from the text. Next ask a person from each pair to share one piece of AHA!

After Reading –

- Model text evidence questions: Spend 5 minutes here
- Show the question: Who is the Hare saluting and talking to when he comes to the water hole a second time? - Answer: A
    - a) Dummy-image
    - b) Himself
    - c) The other animals
    - d) The bird
- Then ask: Where in the text supports your answer? - Answer: Paragraph 15

Ticket out the Door: Spend 5 minutes here

Measure to determine if students understand and can do the skills of the three standards:

Display the question: According to the text, why do you think the animals were so outraged about the Hare coming to the hole?

Grade 9-12 Lesson Plan: *Long-lasting Chemicals May Harm Sea Turtles*
By Brett Israel and Environmental Health News
Retrieved from http://www.environmentalhealthnews.org/ehs/news/2013/toxic-turtles
Created by Lisa Fisher with High School Science Teacher

Standards:
1.   Introduction of Ecology – SC.912.L.17.8 – How do humans impact diversity?
Lesson Essential Question:
1.   How can we make a positive impact on preserving our environment?
Assessment (formative/summative):
1.   Letter to Congressman
Frontload Vocabulary: *Direct students to locate and circle the word as you discuss them.*
1.   contaminate (paragraph 1)
2.   evade (paragraph 2)
3.   treacherous (paragraph 2)
4.   migration (paragraph 2)
5.   neurological (paragraph 4)
Cold Read – [Time yourself – 10-12 minutes]
1.   Number your paragraphs!
2.   Read the text independently and think about the topic and what the author wants you to know about the topic.
Partner Discussion: Have students turn to a shoulder partner and share their literal understanding of the text. Then share out whole class.

Appendix B

Expert Read – [Time yourself – 10-12 minutes]
1. Give partners a different reading perspective:
a. Question Focus: What inferences can you make for possible solutions due to evidence in the text demonstrating not enough is being done?
i. So pull out evidence that makes us believe not enough is being done?
ii. So what can be done to make it happen?
b. OR: Have them highlight in different color the perspective they are assigned/chosen.
Partner Discussion: Have students turn to a shoulder partner and share their highlighted perspective and why. Then share out whole class.
Ticket Out the Door:
1. Letter to congressman
a. Pick one driving piece of evidence to support the solution they are proposing, which will be written in a letter format. Cite *evidence* to be right.

Appendix C
Reading Closely:
Preview/Review Planning Template

Standards:
1. _____
2. _____
3. _____
4. _____

Lesson Essential Question/Learning Target:
1. _____

Assessment (formative/summative):
1. _____

Front-Load Vocabulary:
1. _____
2. _____
3. _____
4. _____
5. _____

Preview (include text features): [Time yourself—_____ minutes]

- **Number your paragraphs!**
- Read the title and author.
- Look over and read any graphs, charts, pictures, captions, etc.
- Highlight key vocabulary (bold/italics).
- Read the entire first paragraph.
- Read the first sentence of each additional paragraph.

- Read the entire last paragraph.
    - Ask the students—
        - What is the topic?
            - _____
        - What does the author want you to know about the topic?
            - _____

Review—Cold Read: [Time yourself—_____ minutes]

1. Students independently read the text for the first time all the way through.
2. When they are done, have them answer literal understanding questions:
    a. What is the text about?
    b. Who is the text about?
    c. Where does the text take place?
    d. When does the text take place?
    e. What is the text structure of the text?

Partner Discussion: Have students turn to a shoulder partner and share their literal understanding of the text. Then share out whole class.

Review—Expert Read: [Time yourself—_____ minutes]

1. Students independently reread the text and create a "table of contents" in the margins that summarizes, pulls out key details/text structures, or highlights information that helps students work toward mastery of the standard(s) and the critical meaning of the text.
2. When they are done, students should be able to use their marginal notes "table of contents" to discuss the critical understanding of the text.
    a. How are the details used to support the author's main idea?

b. How does the text structure support the author's purpose for writing the text?
    c. Why does the author provide the information in this text?
    d. What inferences can you make and how does the text support those conclusions?
Partner Discussion: Have students turn to a shoulder partner and share their critical understanding of the text. Then share out whole class.

Comprehension Questions:
1. _____
    a. Cite *evidence* to be right.
2. _____
    a. Cite *evidence* to be right.
3. _____
    a. Cite *evidence* to be right.

Appendix D
3–12 Sample Reading Closely Lessons

Grade 4 Lesson Plan: Changing Motion
Retrieved from Greatsource Education Group Inc. (2004). *ScienceSaurus: A Student Handbook, Grades 4-5*, Boston: Houghton Mifflin Harcourt.
Created by Andrea Altman, Elementary Literacy Leader

LEARNING TARGETS

Science Big Idea 13: Forces and Changes in Motion

- Identify familiar forces that cause objects to move, including gravity on falling objects.
- Describe that the greater the force applied to it, the greater change in motion of a given object.
- Describe that the more mass an object has, the less effect a given force will have on the object's motion.

Embedded ELA Common Core

- Standard 1: Quote accurately from a text when explaining what the text says explicitly and when drawing inferences from the text.
- Standard 2: Determine two or more main ideas of a text and explain how they are supported by key details; summarize the text.
- Standard 3: Explain the relationships or interactions between two or more individuals, events, ideas, or concepts in a historical, scientific, or technical text based on specific information in the text.

Appendix D

PREVIEW

1. Number your paragraphs.
2. Front-load vocabulary: inertia—the tendency of an object to resist change (par. 3, sent. 1), acceleration—a change in an object's speed or direction (par. 3, sent. 3), gravity—a force that pulls one object toward another (par. 8, sent. 1) *(Students will have these terms defined in the text as well.)*
3. Preview the text.
   a. Read the title and the author.
   b. Pay attention to pictures.
   c. Read the first paragraph.
   d. Read the first sentence of paragraphs 2–9.
   e. Finally, read the last paragraph.
   f. What is the topic?
4. Students turn to a partner and share the topic. Then the teacher asks for a volunteer to share out with the class. What is the topic? *(How motion changes)* What does the author want us to know about the topic? *(There are multiple factors that can change the motion of an object)* (Record on chart paper.)

REVIEW

5. Students do their "cold read." Students will underline what impacts motion for each paragraph. Give students about six minutes to read.
6. Students turn to a partner and discuss their findings. Each pair shares out to the class. Teacher records the students' understanding on chart paper. Number 1–10 to represent paragraphs in the text. *1) a change in motion means starting, stopping, slowing down, or speeding up, 2) a force must act to begin or change motion, 3) inertia means to resist change and acceleration means to change motion, 4) push or pull (force) changes motion, 5) the amount of force impacts the amount of change, 6) the mass of an object impacts the amount of force, 7) forces can combine to change motion, 8) gravity is a force that changes motion, 9) gravity impacts objects of the same size and shape in the same way, 10) gravity has different effects on objects of different shapes.*

7. Expert read: Students create a table of contents summarizing each paragraph in five words or less. Students share their findings/summaries with a partner.
8. Answer questions using table of contents. Teacher models first question using the TOC. The class does the second one as a group as students help think through using the TOC to find the answer. Third question, work with a partner and "cite to be right" using the TOC. The last question is independent. *Come back together to talk about the answer and the "why" behind the answer.*
9. Ticket out the door—What factors impact motion? Use evidence from the text to support your answer.

Grade 9-12 Lesson Plan: *Researchers Say Sun Cycle Alters Earth's Climate* By Nancy Atkinson

Retrieved from http://www.universetoday.com/38454/researchers-say-sun-cycle-alters-earths-climate/

Created by Lisa Fisher

Standards: 1. SC.912.E.5.4 2. SC.912.E.5.5 3. SC.912.E.5.6
Lesson Essential Question: [introduce 2 minutes] 1. How does the sun's dynamic nature connect to the conditions and events on Earth?
Assessment (formative/summative): 1. Ticket out the door
Front-Load Vocabulary: [5 minutes] 1. atmospheric (para. 1, sent. 2)—adj. describes the air or climate in a particular place. 2. stratosphere (para. 1, sent. 3)—n. second layer of the atmosphere. 3. ozone (para. 4, sent. 1)—n. O-oxygen; found in the atmosphere; corrosive; absorbs ultraviolet rays. 4. mechanism (para. 5, sent. 2)—n. the structure or arrangement of parts. 5. equatorial (para. 6, sent. 1)—adj. central. 6. La Niña (para. 6, sent. 1)—a cooling of the surface water of the eastern and central Pacific Ocean (not as frequent as and is the opposite of El Niño). 7. El Niño (para. 7, sent. 2)—a warm ocean current of variable intensity that develops after late December.

Preview (include text features): [Time yourself—3 minutes]
- **Number your paragraphs!**
- Read the title and author.
- Look over and read any graphs, charts, pictures, captions, etc.
- Highlight key vocabulary (bold/italics).
- Read the entire first paragraph.
- Read the first sentence of each additional paragraph.
- Read the entire last paragraph.
    o **Ask the students—**
        ▪ What is the topic?
            • Sun's cycle
        ▪ What does the author want you to know about the topic?
            • Variations of the sun cycle have effects on Earth's climate.

Review—Cold Read: [Time yourself—6 minutes]
1. Students independently read the text for the first time all the way through.
2. When they are done, have them answer literal understanding questions:
    a. What is the text about?
        i. Variation in the sun's energy/cycle
    b. What is the author's purpose for writing this article?
        i. To inform readers of advances on predicting the sun's impact on Earth's

      c. Where does the text take place?
           i. Atmosphere layers of Earth
      d. What is the text structure/pattern relationship of the text?
           i. Cause/effect

Partner Discussion: [2 minutes]
Have students turn to a shoulder partner and share their literal understanding of the text. Then share out whole class.

Review—Expert Read: [Time yourself—6 minutes]
1. Students independently reread the text and create a "table of contents" in the margins that summarizes, pulls out key details, or highlights information that helps students work toward mastery of the standard(s) and the critical meaning of the text.
2. When they are done, students should be able to use their marginal notes "table of contents" to discuss the critical understanding of the text.
      a. How are the details used to support the author's main idea?
      b. How does the text structure support the author's purpose for writing the text?
      c. Why does the author provide the information in this text?
      d. What inferences can you make, and how does the text support those conclusions?

Partner Discussion: [2 minutes]
Have students turn to a shoulder partner and share their critical understanding of the text. Then share out whole class.

Comprehension Questions: [5 minutes]
1. According to the text, in what ways does the sun's cycle impact Earth?
      a. Cite *evidence* to be right.

Appendix E
Blank Ticket Out the Door

Ticket Out the Door

Name _____ Date _____

Ticket Out the Door

Name _____ Date _____

Appendix F
*Reading Closely:
Strategic Approach Planning Template*

Standards:

1. _____

2. _____

3. _____

4. _____

Lesson Essential Question/Learning Target:

1. _____

Assessment (formative/summative):

1. _____

Lesson Planning Steps:

1. Set the purpose for reading (before reading)—

    a. Question/quick write/anticipation guide:

    _____

2. **Number your paragraphs!**

3. Front-load vocabulary (before reading)—

    a. _____

    b. _____

    c. _____

    d. _____

    e. _____

4. Cold read—(Time yourself—_____ minutes)

    a. Connect purpose to essential question to mark the text (during reading):

Appendix F

        i. _____

        ii. _____

        iii. _____

Partner Discussion:

5. Expert read—(Time yourself—_____ minutes)
   a. Categorize text marking to begin to formulate a position/stance/point of view—
      i. Categories should connect to purpose and essential question (during reading):
         1. _____
         2. _____
         3. _____
         4. _____

Partner Discussion:

6. Answer essential question using evidence from the text—
   i. Should include text marking within the category that answers the question:
   _____

Appendix G
3–12 Sample Reading Closely Lessons

Grade 7 Lesson Plan: Civic
Retrieved from http://www.nytimes.com/2010/03/30/us/30bully.html?page
   wanted=all&_r=0
Created by Lisa Fisher

Standards:

1. SS.7.C.2.4—Evaluate rights contained in the Bill of Rights and other amendments to the Constitution.

2. SS.7.C.3.6—Evaluate constitutional rights and their impact on individuals and society.

Lesson Essential Question:

1. How do the amendments prevent the civil rights of human beings from being violated?

Assessment (formative/summative):

1. Mini quiz

Lesson Planning Steps:

1. Set the purpose for reading (before reading)—
    a. Activator: How important is it to have your rights protected by laws?
        i. Extremely
        ii. Somewhat
        iii. Not at all

2. **Number your paragraphs!**

3. Front-load vocabulary (before reading)—
    a. indictments
    b. statutory rape
    c. taunting
    d. prosecutor
    e. civil versus criminal (felony)

4. Cold read—(Time yourself—8 minutes)
    a. Think about this question during reading and mark details in the text: What

actions are discussed throughout the article that represent an amendment?

   i. 1st Amendment

   ii. 5th Amendment

   iii. 6th Amendment

   iv. 8th Amendment

   v. 14th Amendment

Partner Discussion: Share your text marking and reasoning with a shoulder partner.

5. Expert read—(Time yourself—8 minutes)

   a. Categorize the text markings based on the question *What evidence from the text provides information to help you understand each amendment?*

      i. Freedom

      ii. Due process

      iii. Lawyer

      iv. Punishment

      v. Discrimination

Partner Discussion: Share with your shoulder partner how you categorized the details from the text.

6. Respond to questions about the text:

   a. What right was violated in the case of Phoebe Prince? *(Answer: She wanted to go to school free from the harassment of bullies.)*

   b. Do you agree that this case was a violation of a teen right? Why or why not?

   c. The article mentions that Phoebe Prince recently came to the United States from Ireland. In your opinion, what role did this fact play in the violation of her rights?

      i. Do you know of any other instances of teen rights being violated because of race or ethnicity?

Appendix G

Grade 4 Lesson Plan: Ponce de Leon
Retrieved from http://www.readinga-z.com/
Created by Lisa Fisher

Standards:

SS.4.A.3.1 Identify explorers who came to Florida and the motivations for their expeditions.

SS.4.A.3.2 Describe causes and effects of European colonization on the Native American tribes of Florida.

Embedded ELA

RI.4.1 Refer to details and examples in a text when explaining what the text says explicitly and when drawing inferences from the text.

RI.4.2 Determine the main idea of a text and explain how it is supported by key details; summarize the text.

RI.4.3 Explain events, procedures, ideas, or concepts in a historical, scientific, or technical text, including what happened and why, based on specific information in the text.

Essential Question (EQ):

How have Native American tribes and European exploration influenced Florida?

Assessment (formative/summative):

Students will answer the questions and answer the EQ Handout as well as be able to do the categorization handout. This will help us know if students are being successful in working towards the standard.

Lesson Planning Steps:

Set the Purpose for Reading (before reading) –

  a. Question connected to EQ: Based on your current understanding, how important is exploration in your life?

  i. Very important

  ii. Somewhat important

  iii. Not important

2. Frontload Vocabulary (before reading) –

  a. colonize – to settle an area (par. 3 sentence 4)

  b. mythical – story not based in fact (par. 4 sentence 3)

  c. encountered – meet; came upon (par. 6 sentence 2)

  d. current – a large body of water moving in a certain direction (par. 6 sentence 2)

  e. ambush – unexpected attack (par. 9 sentence 4)

3. Cold Read –

  a. Think about this question during text marking: What was successful about Ponce de Leon's explorations and how were they threatened?

  i. S – Successes of Ponce de Leon's explorations

  ii. T – Threats to Ponce de Leon's explorations

Partner Discussion: Partner 1 tells Partner 2 what successes Ponce de Leon had. Partner 2 tells Partner 1 what threats Ponce de Leon encountered. If there are differences, discuss why. Students share out to the class as teacher records thoughts on chart paper.

4. Expert Read –

  a. Think about this question when taking text markings and categorizing those

details: Which of the following was the driving force behind early exploration?
 	
    i. Land
    ii. Resources
    iii. Power
 	
Partner Discussion: Partners compare their notes and discuss how they categorized their evidence and what they think is the driving force behind early exploration.

5. Answer the EQ with supporting details from text marking and drawing conclusions with categorizations: According to the text, how does exploration change native lands? Rubric 3 points – identify 2 ways exploration changes native lands and supports using evidence from the text 2 points – identify 1 way exploration changes native lands and supports using evidence from the text 1 point – identify 1 way exploration changes native lands

Appendix H
Evidence Log

Text/Author	Detail (para./pg.)	Triangulated (supported)	Inquiry Needed	New Source	Validated/Negated Evidence

Appendix I
Analyzing Craft and Structure of Text

Appendix I

Literacy	Structure	Point of View	Purpose	Tone
Text 1:	Evidence:	Evidence:	Evidence:	Evidence:
Text 2:	Evidence:	Evidence:	Evidence:	Evidence:
Text 3:	Evidence	Evidence:	Evidence:	Evidence:

Appendix J
Literary Text by Content Topic

BUSINESS, COMMUNICATION, AND TECHNOLOGY—TEACHING DIGITAL CITIZENSHIP

- *Wonder* by R. J. Palacio (fiction)—790 Lexile
- *Schooled* by Gordon Korman (fiction)—740 Lexile
- *The Misfits* by James Howe (fiction)—960 Lexile
- *Dark Days of Hamburger Halpin* by Josh Berk (fiction)—820 Lexile
- *The Revealers* by Doug Wilhelm (fiction)—580 Lexile
- *Bystanders* by James Preller (fiction)—600 Lexile
- *Out of My Mind* by Sharon Draper (fiction)—700 Lexile
- *The Skin I'm In* by Sharon Flake (fiction)—670 Lexile
- *Stepping on the Cracks* by Mary Downing Hahn (fiction)—780 Lexile
- *The Truth about Truman School* by Dori Hillestad Butler (fiction)—640 Lexile

CIVICS—RIGHTS AND RESPONSIBILITIES

- *Among the Hidden* by Margaret Haddix—800 Lexile
- *Hidden in Plain Sight: The Tragedy of Children's Rights from Ben Franklin to Lionel Tate* by Barbara Bennett Woodhouse
- *Fredrick Douglass: Young Defender of Human Rights* by Elisabeth P. Myers
- *The Watsons Go to Birmingham* by Christopher Paul Curtis—1000 Lexile
- *The Outsiders* by S. E. Hinton—750 Lexile

- *The Giver* by Lois Lowry—760 Lexile
- *To Kill a Mockingbird* by Harper Lee—870 Lexile
- *Spies of Mississippi* by Rick Bowers—1290 Lexile
- *Copper Sun* by Sharon Draper—820 Lexile
- *Abraham Lincoln, Slavery, and the Civil War* by Michael Johnson—980 Lexile
- *Through My Eyes* by Ruby Bridges—860 Lexile

SOCIAL STUDIES—CONFLICT AND DESTRUCTION

- *The Diary of a Young Girl* by Anne Frank—1080 Lexile
- *I Will Plant You a Lilac Tree: A Memoir of a Schindler's List Survivor* by Laura Hillman—740 Lexile
- *Night* by Elie Wiesel—570 Lexile
- *I Survived the Bombing of Pearl Harbor, 1941* by Lauren Tarshis—620 Lexile
- *Farewell to Manzanar* by Jeanne Houston and James Houston—1040 Lexile
- *The City of Ember* by Jeanne Duprau—680 Lexile
- *Candor* by Pam Bachorz—HL 350
- *The Compound* by S. A. Bodeen—570 Lexile
- *September 11, 2001: Attack on New York City* by Wilborn Hampton—1060 Lexile

Professional References

ACT. (2006). *Reading between the lines: What the ACT reveals about college readiness in reading.* ACT, Inc.

Calkins, L., Ehrenworth, M., & Lehman, C. (2012). *Pathways to the common core: Accelerating achievement.* Portsmouth, NH: Heinemann.

Common Core State Standards Initiative. (2012). *Common core state standards initiative: Preparing America's students for college & career.* Retrieved March 18, 2012 from http://www.corestandards.org/the-standards.

Florida Department of Education. (2012). Collaborate plan align learn motivate share (CPALMS). National Science Foundation and FCR-STEM. Retrieved August 8, 2011 from http://www.cpalms.org/homepage/index.aspx.

U. S. Department of Education, Institute of Education Sciences, National Center for Education Statistics, National Assessment of Educational Progress (NAEP). (2011). The nation's report card: Reading 2011, national assessment of educational progress at grades 4 and 8. Retrieved from http://nces.ed.gov/nationsreportcard/pdf/main2011/2012457.pdf.

Literature References

Anderson, Laurie Halse. (2000). *Fever 1793*. New York: Scholastic.

Masoff, Joy. (2004). "Bacteria: The Good, the Bad, and the Stinky" in *Read-Aloud Anthology* by Janet Allen and Patrick Daley. New York: Scholastic.

Preston, Richard. (2002). Excerpt from *The Demon in the Freezer: A True Story*. New York: Random House.

EyeWitness to History. (2001). *The Black Death, 1348*. Retrieved from www.eyewitnesstohistory.com on August 1, 2011.

About the Author

Lisa Fisher is a full-time literacy specialist for Pasco County Schools in Florida and an independent consultant for literacy trainings and workshops along the East Coast. In both capacities she inspires educators to work with students to read and write critically about a wide range of texts. She is a literacy leader with a passion for encouraging all educators to help the struggling and reluctant learners find success. Fisher's other professional writings include *Surviving the Move and Learning to Thrive: Tools for Success in Secondary Schools, Grades 6–12* (2011), *Read, Discuss, and Learn: Using Literacy Groups to Student Advantage* (2010), and a chapter entitled "A Splash of Color with a Dash of Discovery Makes One Great Shade" in *Empowering the Voice of the Teacher Researcher: Achieving Success through a Culture of Inquiry*, edited by Roger Brindley and Christine Crocco (2009). Educators can stay connected by visiting her blog, http://lisafisher2003.edublogs.org, or website, http://lisafisher.org. She continues to reside in Florida with her husband and four Chihuahuas.

www.ingramcontent.com/pod-product-compliance
Lightning Source LLC
Chambersburg PA
CBHW081828300426
44116CB00014B/2510